A Matter of Faith

To my friend
Cat —
Rejoice in the
Lord always!,
love you,
Carol

Why I Chose this Cover

Some may ask why I chose this particular photo for my book cover. If you recall the famous poem "Footprints in the Sand," you will remember that the poet had questions about the number of footprints in the sand. Sometimes there were two sets of prints, other times there was one only. When the poet asks the Lord about this, He replies, "The years when you have seen only one set of footprints, my child, is when I carried you."

There was something intriguing about this particular photo. Then, I realized why. When we choose not to follow in the Lord's footsteps, we miss God's best for our lives. It is my prayer that the enclosed selections of my weekly faith-based columns will inspire you to walk with Him.

Carol Round

A Matter of Faith

Carol Round

Buoy Up
Press

Denton Texas

Buoy Up Press
An imprint of AWOC.COM Publishing
P.O. Box 2819
Denton, TX 76202

Manufactured in the United States of America

ISBN: 978-0-937660-45-4

Table of Contents

For My Faithful Friends

"Two are better than one, because they have a good reward for their labor; For if they fall, the one will lift up his fellow. But woe to him who is alone when he falls and has not another to lift him up!" Ecclesiastes 4:9-10

How amazing is our Lord who would see to it that our paths cross with those who make a difference in our lives. I am so blessed by the women of faith who have crossed my path, not by chance, but by His perfect plan.

In no particular order:

Clarice Doyle, Charlie Shotsky, Melissa Holt, Sharon Koons, Janelle Brammer, Dorothy Willman, Jana Christian, Jennifer Kirby, Myrtle Prather, Alice Benalice, Michelle Gourd, Roma Estes, Barbara Beck, Jeanette Standfield and my dear Patti Eastland, who went home to be with the Lord on December 24, 2007

Too Many Presents Under the Tree

"He has scattered abroad his gifts to the poor, his righteousness endures forever; his horn will be lifted high in honor." Psalms 112:9

I was not surprised when I heard Christmas carols playing in a local store; however, I was dismayed because it was only two days after Halloween. What happened to Thanksgiving?

I went to that same local store yesterday to buy some soaker hoses because I needed to water my foundation. They didn't have any in their garden center. Prices were being lowered to get rid of merchandise to make room for the Christmas decorations that were already threatening to jump off the shelves and strangle you if you refused to acknowledge their presence on that unusually warm November day. Sure didn't feel like Christmas to me.

I commented to the store clerk who was assisting me that it seemed like the stores were more eager than ever to display their Christmas finery. Next thing you know they'll be advertising the holiday season right after the fourth of July, I told her. She replied that she would not be surprised if it became a year-round event. She agreed that it was a bit of overkill. Like me, she wondered what has happened to Thanksgiving.

As we rush into this holiday season once again, some of us forget to give thanks for the blessings that we already have. For many this Christmas—as in years past—there will be nothing under the tree on December 25. Many will wake up to a cold home because they cannot afford to pay their utility bills let alone buy gifts.

Although I like receiving gifts, opening a beautifully wrapped package is not nearly as fulfilling as the times that I have given of myself, my money, and my time to help others in need. As college students, my roommate, Mary, and I adopted four siblings during the Christmas season. The children were close in age: two, four, six and seven. Their parents struggled to just get by. Armed with a shopping list, Mary and I found that shopping for our adopted children was one of our most rewarding college experiences.

It was a joy to take the four to eat at the college cafeteria. We might have complained about the food—mystery meat again—but those kids sure didn't. Afterwards, we took them to the college-wide Christmas program where Santa handed out gifts to each child in attendance. The children were in awe of the decorated Christmas tree that reached to the ceiling of the college gymnasium. I still don't know where the college found a tree that tall but I do know that the excitement on those little faces lit up my life that cold December night.

When was the last time that you looked beyond the glitter of the holiday season to see the true meaning that can be found in sharing with others? Are there too many presents under your tree? Let the Lord direct you to those who are in greater need.

Cultivating a Heart of Gratitude

"Give thanks to the LORD, for he is good; his love endures forever." Psalms 107:1

Although it has been about three months since Hurricane Katrina and her sister, Rita, hit the gulf coast area, victims are still in need. The death toll is well over 1,000 and bodies are still being recovered. Over one million people were displaced. Most cannot return to their homes because they are uninhabitable.

For those of us who were not directly affected by the most devastating natural disaster in U.S. history, it is easy to forget, as time passes, that there are people who still need our prayers and assistance. Because we are constantly bombarded by the media with bad news, we seem to develop immunity to suffering.

A friend emailed me an online journal that was kept by her granddaughter who lives in Cypress, a suburb just northwest of Houston, Texas. Forecasters had predicted that Houston would receive the biggest hit from Hurricane Rita.

Rachel's family chose to ride out the hurricane. Her email journal entries, to keep her family in Oklahoma informed, covered the hours and days leading up to the expected arrival of Hurricane Rita as well as the aftermath. About their preparations and those of her neighbors, she wrote: "We are fortunate. With any major storm, you prepare for the worst and let God do the rest."

However, the Houston area was spared the brunt of Rita. Filled with thanksgiving, Rachel wrote, "Pray for those less fortunate. Cherish each day. Find something to smile about—even if it the fact that God has a purpose for giving you one more day upon this earth. Use it for Him."

Although Rita spared the lives of many in the Louisiana and Texas area, the victims of Katrina were not so blessed. Victims from both disasters have emerged with stories of gratitude. They are just grateful to be alive, to have an opportunity to start over, to have one more day on earth.

As Rachel wrote her online journal, she commented to her family on things that many of us in our busy lives take for granted. She wrote: "Some wind and rain…northerly gusts of tropical air…good for the lungs. Power remained…only a few outages in the area."

How can we cultivate an attitude of gratitude when we take everyday things like electricity and water coming out of the tap for granted? To cultivate means "to grow or tend or to promote the growth of." That means we have to consciously make the decision to grow our own attitude of thanksgiving. But, like a plant, we must continue to weed, prune and water it if we want it to flourish.

At the end of each day, make a list of all the things for which you are grateful. It can be ongoing things such as family and friends or your health. If you are having trouble with your list, remember this: It doesn't have to be something large or profound or personal; it just needs to be sincere.

When was the last time you were grateful for the simple things in life that we take for granted? Ask the Lord to help you cultivate a heart of gratitude.

News Matters More Than Ever

"But the angel said to them, do not be afraid. I bring you good news of great joy that will be for all the people." Luke 2:10

I recently saw a billboard proclaiming, "News Matters More Than Ever." I don't recall the company who was using this slogan, but the words stuck with me.

With our media-drenched society, we are bombarded daily from all directions with news—radio, television, newspapers, magazines and the Internet. I am sure there is more technology to deliver the news but I am not that savvy.

I am aware, however, that most of the news we hear on a daily basis can leave us shell-shocked. Shell-shocked, usually associated with combat fatigue, means stunned, distressed, or exhausted from a prolonged trauma or an unexpected difficulty.

We have been stunned and distressed by an extraordinary amount of bad news this past year, beginning with the Asian tsunami last December that killed more than 200,000 people in 13 countries. Thousands more have died or been left homeless because of monster hurricanes in the southern United States and the recent devastating earthquakes in Asia. Daily reports remind us that the devastation is still taking a toll on lives. Headlines also report the loss of more lives in the Iraqi war.

No one is immune to the effects of these disasters or war. Our backyard may not be the setting but the results are the same. We are left with questions. How could a loving God let this happen? Could it have been prevented? What could we do to make sure this doesn't happen again? Who is to blame?

Even if we don't know someone who has lost a loved one or property in these disasters, we are all indirectly affected. When gas prices skyrocketed to an all-time high, the media constantly reminded us of the bad news. I was filling up my tank one day during the volatile ten cents per day jump in prices. I, like many others, found temporary comfort in complaining with others about the high prices as we filled our tanks. This particular day, I was reminded that for some the bad news of rising gas prices could be devastating.

A woman, filling up her tank at the next pump, said, "I don't know how much longer I can even afford to drive to work. I make minimum wage." She was nearly in tears. My heart went out to her as she replaced the nozzle and drove away.

We can't drive away from bad news. We can't escape the fact that there will always be natural and man-made disasters that are out of our control.

We can, however, embrace the Good News that was delivered over 2,000 years ago to shepherds watching over their flocks in a field. If we listen carefully, we can hear the angel of the Lord announcing the birth of a child who would bring hope to the world. It is news that will bring joy from your head to your toes.

He is our hope. Have you heard the Good News? If not, seek the One who is the deliverer of good news. His news matters more than ever.

Getting Spiritually Fit

"Forgetting what is behind and straining toward what is ahead, I press on toward the goal to win the prize for which God has called me heavenward in Jesus Christ." Philippians 3:13-14

Lose weight. Get healthy. Quit smoking. Save more money. Spend more time with family. All are worthy resolutions.

When we turn the calendar to a new year, we usually reflect on where we have been and where we want to be. We look at our failures and ask ourselves, "What do I need to change?"

A friend and I recently disagreed about failure. His views about failure have created eyes that see the world through cynical glasses. I believe that failure is an opportunity for growth.

You don't continue to beat a dead horse but neither do you leave him lying beside the road. Pretty soon he begins to stink.

I've heard people say, "I have no regrets about my life. If I had it to do over again, I'd do it the same way."

Not me. Although I don't wallow in the pool of regret, I'd definitely do some things differently.

We can learn from our failures to become the person that God created us to be. To do that, we have to look at the past—and that requires confession. Confession is powerful. Owning up to failure is the first, painful step on the path to something better.

Changing the calendar to a new year is a good time for a spiritual checkup.

When you see a new calendar, do you see days and months of blank spaces ready to be filled in with God's plans for your life or do you see a busy schedule that is taking you away from Him?

Is your life producing something of value for God?

Do you trust Him instead of relying on your own strength and understanding?

Is there something in your life that is holding you back from all that God has waiting for you?

Are you open to God's leading?

There is no magic pill that transforms us—either physically or spiritually. It requires a plan and if we fail to plan, then we plan to fail—a cliché, but true.

Becoming spiritually mature is simply a matter of learning certain spiritual exercises. Just like getting physically fit requires exercise, we must become self-disciplined in our spiritual lives. To shape our character, we must take the time to develop good habits.

Pastor Rick Warren, the author of the best-seller, *A Purpose Driven Life*, says that to develop spiritual fitness, our daily habits must include time spent with God, prayer, Bible reading and obedience to what He reveals to you.

Becoming spiritually mature involves more than a quick fix. In our instant gratification society, we want it now—nuke it in the microwave for five minutes and it's done. But growing spiritually is a gradual process.

Taking the time to grow spiritually is a lifetime endeavor. Are you willing to make the commitment? It requires patience. Knowing that God isn't finished with us yet, we must press on toward the goal.

I Think I Can, I Think I Can

"Are you so foolish? After beginning with the Spirit, are you now trying to attain your goal by human effort?" Galatians 3:3

Another year has come and gone. As we write checks to pay our bills, we have to remind ourselves that it is now 2006.

For 12 months we have written 2005 without thinking. As the days pass, we will forget the old year and our hand will automatically correct our thoughts. Wouldn't it be nice if the rest of our life was like that?

When a new year arrives, our thoughts turn to new beginnings. We set goals and vow to make changes.

Although writing a new year on our checks easily becomes a habit, it takes self-discipline to stick with our goals. Many people avoid that word: self-discipline. They claim, "I have no will power."

The will has no power. We have to seek a power greater than ourselves to achieve long-term success with goals.

Dr. Charles Stanley, pastor and president of In Touch Ministries, says a self-disciplined life must involve pleasing the Lord.

To make change a permanent part of our lives—the kind of change that improves our lives and the lives of others—we must have definite, specific goals. Writing those goals down requires us to evaluate our lives and our dreams. Goals, says Dr. Stanley, are merely statements of faith.

We can't focus on our future without setting our sights on our goals. Then, says Dr. Stanley, we have to pursue discipline with diligence.

Remember the story of The Little Engine that Could? The story actually had its roots in 1906 in a Sunday School publication, *Wellsprings for Young People*. As the story goes, a little railroad engine was asked to pull a long train of freight cars over a hill after a larger engine said, "I can't."

The little engine puffed bravely up the hill, faster and faster, as he chanted, "I think I can, I think I can, I think I can."

Sometimes we are faced with a mountain that seems insurmountable but like that little red engine, we have to focus on the ultimate goal—doing our best and being our best with the tools the Lord has given us. He may ask us to do things that seem beyond our abilities but He will always equip us for the task at hand.

When our aim is valid and we are willing to pay the price, God will grace us with the strength and direction to accomplish worthy goals.

Ask yourself: Where do I lack self-discipline? Why am I having trouble reaching my goals? Do I have a firm sense of direction? Do I have a clear picture and a consuming desire to reach those goals? Do I have a course of action and a cooperative spirit? Do I have the courage to act?

What worthy goals is the Lord asking you to accomplish today? With a confidence in God and yourself, you can be like that little engine. I think I can, I think I can.

Are You Suffering From Stuffitis?

"Where your treasure is, there your heart will be also."
Matthew 6:21

Do you suffer from "stuffitis?"

What on earth is that? Is it contagious? Is it serious? Is there a cure?

First of all, let me define this disease. People who suffer from "stuffitis" are always collecting stuff. And no matter how much they collect, it is never enough. They think it is a cure for everything that ails them, especially unhappiness. They get a temporary high—a feel-good feeling—that lasts until the bills come in.

Secondly, "stuffitis" can be contagious. When we buy things to "keep up with the Joneses," then we have bought into the American lie—that more and bigger stuff will make us happy, make us the envy of the neighborhood, make us better than others.

Third, "stuffitis" is serious because it is the inability to appreciate what we have and an unending desire to have more. We go into debt with easily-obtained credit to buy more and more stuff. Then when we become bored with that stuff or think we need better stuff, we charge even more.

Eventually, this preoccupation with buying more stuff can lead to financial failure. U.S. consumer bankruptcies increased to a record 2.04 million in 2005, as people rushed to seek protection from creditors ahead of tough new laws, according to recently released data.

Collecting stuff until it overruns our homes and lives is an addiction; however, it is curable. It is a painful process. But freeing yourself from this disease allows peace to enter your life and your home.

My problem is that I like a bargain and when there is a sale, I head right for the racks of marked-down items. My adrenaline begins to pump when I see that perfect pair of shoes or a blouse that would go with my favorite skirt. It is something that I have to fight because I have way too many clothes and shoes in my closet.

Armed recently with a $25 gift certificate to one of my favorite department stores, I knew what I needed when I went inside. Notice, I said needed, as in necessary, not desired. After I used my gift certificate to purchase my necessities, I wandered over to the shoe department. I was thrilled to see that the winter boots, which were already half-price, had been marked down another 40 percent.

I tried on several pairs—six to be exact. I would have had to pay less than $25 for the pair that I liked, if I had bought them. I didn't. I placed all of the boxes back on the display shelf and browsed through the racks of running shoes. I really need running shoes, not boots. But I'm waiting for them to go on sale.

How often do we confuse want with need? How often do we let our desires for more, more, more lead to a life of financial ruin?

God promises us an abundant life. An abundant life, however, is one filled with Him. If our life is filled with too much stuff, how can we make room for Him?

Does your lifestyle honor the Lord or have you become afflicted with "stuffitis?"

The Ultimate Makeover

But the Lord said to Samuel, "Do not consider his appearance or his height, for I have rejected him. The Lord does not look at the things man looks at. Man looks at the outward appearance, but the Lord looks at the heart." Isaiah 16:7

Check out the cover of just about any magazine at the local supermarket and the headlines seem to taunt you: "Lose 25 pounds in 6 Weeks;" "Ten Ways to Find Happiness;" "Find the Love of your Life in 30 days."

As a society we are obsessed by perfection. We seek the perfect job, the perfect body, the perfect mate.

Reality shows like "Extreme Makeover"—not the home edition—and "Wife Swap" are examples of dissatisfaction with ourselves and our lives. An extreme makeover is good for the self-esteem of those who undergo such a dramatic physical change. We all want to look our best. But looking our best and being our best are not the same.

As a child, I was shy, a bookworm. I was not athletically inclined. In a society that values physical prowess over other personal attributes, I didn't fit. In elementary school, when teams were formed for dodge ball or some other sport, I was chosen last. Being chosen last colored my view of myself. I longed to be the most athletic, the team captain, the one who did the choosing.

I suffered from low self-esteem. Then, in my mid-forties, a friend and I started a power-walking program which eventually led to competing in 5K races as a runner. I won a trophy for my age division in my first race.

Bitten by the racing bug, I took up the challenge of the Tulsa Run. By this time, I was no longer competing against others to win. I was competing against myself. Could I reach my personal goal to finish the race in 90 minutes?

I was encouraged by several friends who helped me pace myself during the 12-mile race. I was disappointed when, three miles from the finish line, I developed a side cramp and was forced to walk. However, through encouragement from a 75-year-old race master, I was able to sprint to the finish line.

Although I didn't win a trophy—which was not my goal—I finished in 97 minutes. It was my personal best. I knew before I started the race that I would never achieve perfection by coming in first, but I knew that it didn't matter. I had done my personal best.

Our relationship with God is like that race. With His encouragement, He wants us to reach the finish line. He wants us to be our personal best. He doesn't look at our outside. He doesn't see the crooked teeth or nose or other physical flaws as we do. He wants to do an extreme makeover from the inside out.

Are you ready for the most extreme makeover of your life? Look in the mirror and see the person that He does. Ask for God's guidance to change your life from the inside out. The only extreme makeover we need is finding our best selves through a personal relationship with Him

Keep Love Alive

"This is love: not that we loved God, but that he loved us and sent his Son as an atoning sacrifice for our sins." 1 John 4:10

Valentine's Day is over. The flowers are probably wilted. The candy is almost gone. The helium-filled balloons are not floating as high. The euphoria of a day that celebrates love has faded.

What does love mean? The American Heritage Dictionary offers this definition: "A deep, tender, ineffable feeling of affection and solicitude toward a person, such as that arising from kinship, recognition of attractive qualities, or a sense of underlying oneness."

I recently received the following email with, what I consider much better definitions of love:

A group of professional people posed this question to a group of 4 to 8-year-olds: "What does love mean?" The answers they got were broader and deeper than anyone could have imagined. See what you think:

"When my grandmother got arthritis, she couldn't bend over and paint her toenails anymore. So my grandfather does it for her all the time, even when his hands got arthritis too. That's love." Rebecca- age 8

"Love is when you go out to eat and give somebody most of your French fries without making them give you any of theirs." Chrissy - age 6

"Love is what makes you smile when you're tired." Terri - age 4

"Love is when my mommy makes coffee for my daddy and she takes a sip before giving it to him, to make sure the taste is OK." Danny - age 7

"Love is what's in the room with you at Christmas if you stop opening presents and listen." Bobby - age 7 (Wow!)

"If you want to learn to love better, you should start with a friend who you hate," Nikka - age 6 (We need a few million more Nikka's on this planet.)

"Love is like a little old woman and a little old man who are still friends even after they know each other so well." Tommy - age 6

I think these children have a better grasp of love than the adult writers of the dictionary. Don't you?

Author and lecturer Leo Buscaglia once talked about a contest he was asked to judge. The purpose of the contest was to find the most caring child. The winner was a four-year-old child whose next door neighbor was an elderly gentleman who had recently lost his wife.

Upon seeing the man cry, the little boy went into the old gentleman's yard, climbed onto his lap, and just sat there. When his Mother asked what he had said to the neighbor, the little boy said, "Nothing, I just helped him cry"

Buscaglai, who died in 1998, often said, "God's gift to you is life itself. What you do with it is your gift to God."

After Buscaglai's death, those who appreciated the affect he had on their lives, started a celebration called, "Keep Love Alive."

Are you keeping love alive? When there is nothing left but God that is when you find that God is all you need.

Put Love on Your List

"And now these three remain: faith, hope and love. But the greatest of these is love." 1Corinthians 13

Browsing through a greeting card rack at a local store, I saw this message posted at the end of the rack: "Put love on your list."

My first reaction was: Are we so busy that we have to remember to love? Must we put it on our to-do-list to make room for it in our lives?

In our fast-paced "me-first" society, I guess we do. But shouldn't love be something that comes naturally, without thinking, just doing?

My mother, who is now deceased, was an example. I never remember, as I was growing up, hearing the words, "I love you, Carol," from her lips.

I don't doubt my mother's love. I never did, even if I was over 40-years-old before I heard those words that I longed to hear from her. She showed her love in other ways. She was a stay-at-home mom. She had a warm meal on the table every evening. Eating out was considered a luxury in the 60s or maybe our society was slower-paced and we had more time to sit down at the dinner table for a home-cooked meal.

My mother, also a seamstress, made all of the clothes for my sister and me. Her talents produced dresses that only love could buy.

Mother's love was also evident in the teaching of responsibility. My mother posted a chore list on the refrigerator every Saturday morning. Until our chores were done, my sister and I couldn't go out to play. Did we appreciate the lesson she was teaching us at the time? Probably not.

After my sister and I left home, our mother's love was expressed in new ways: the sharing of recipes, making quilts for grandchildren, preparing large holiday meals for our growing families, and making jelly from wild plums and blackberries that we picked.

When my mother's health began to fail several years ago, her ways of expressing love were no longer possible. The hands that had sewn dresses for my sister and I were gnarled with arthritis. The strong back that had allowed her to stand in the kitchen for hours to prepare a holiday meal or make jelly became bent with osteoporosis.

Eventually, she required round-the-clock care and went to live in a nursing home. I received a call early one morning about two months after she was admitted. The nurse on duty suggested that the family be called.

As I sat by my mother's bedside and watched her breathing become more labored, I stroked her hair and said, "I love you, mama."

She was not conscious but as the hours passed, peacefulness appeared on her face; the 79 years that were evident in the lines on her face disappeared. When she drew her last breath, I saw nothing but the young mother who loved her daughters.

Is love on your to-do list? Ask God to show you who needs your love the most today.

This is the Day that the Lord Has Made

"This is the day the Lord has made; let us rejoice and be glad in it." Psalm 118:24

I recall a summer morning over 25 years ago. My oldest son and I were walking down a country road.

He would stop frequently to poke a small stick into the dirt or a mushroom that had bloomed after an overnight rain.

When he looked up from his inquisitive searching and saw the orange, red and purple sunrise, he exclaimed, "Look Mom, God sure got up early this morning."

"How do you know?" I asked.

"Because he's been busy painting the sky," Casey replied.

I can remember my own Louisiana childhood days. I would spend hours outdoors in the sultry heat. My mother would usually find me lying on my back or on my stomach in the grass.

On my back I could look up at the clouds and imagine what God was doing up there. What did He spend His days doing?

My childish imagination pictured Him with the angels having a contest to see who could come up with the best cloudscape. Did God let them win once in awhile?

On my stomach I would be looking for four-leaf clovers or watching those little-hard-shelled creatures that I called roly-poly bugs. I didn't—and still don't—know their scientific name. I was just captivated by their funny looks. I'd poke them and watch them roll into a little ball for protection from my curious finger.

My fascination with God's wonders didn't end when the sun went down. I can remember firefly hunting with my sister. We would borrow some of mom's Mason jars and poke holes in the lid.

In our eagerness to capture the insects while their lights were on, we would race across the lawn barefooted. More than once, our enthusiastic hunting tactics led to a broken jar and a cut foot.

When the lightning bug hunt was over—usually because mom made us come inside—we would take our nocturnal captives with us. Placing the jars on our windowsill, we would drift to sleep with the tiny insects flashing their lanterns.

It was only later in life that my curiosity led me to do some research on lightning bugs. I learned that their flashing signaled a desire to mate. What I found even more fascinating is that each lightning bug species has its own specific flash pattern so that it doesn't attract a firefly of a different species.

As a child, I didn't care why they were lighting the night skies. I just enjoyed their lightning bug dance.

As an adult I cannot fathom how anyone, who sees a sunrise or sunset, a cloud formation or a four-leaf clover, a roly-poly bug or a firefly, can deny the existence of God.

Even today, when I see a sunrise, I have a vision of God with paintbrush in hand putting His bold strokes on the morning sky.

Have you seen God at work today? Open your eyes and enjoy. He did it all for you.

A Direct Line to God

"Answer me when I call to you, O my righteous God. Give me relief from my distress; be merciful to me and hear my prayer." Psalms 4:1

"Mr. Watson—come here—I want to see you." Who would have thought that these famous first words uttered on March 10, 1876 would change the world?

Alexander Graham Bell's spoken words to his assistant Thomas A. Watson marked the beginning of a whole new wave of communication in our history with the invention of the telephone. By the end of 1880, there were 47,900 telephones in the United States.

Now, fast forward to the 21st century where everyone seems to be walking around with a cell phone in their hands. I swore I'd never get a cell phone. I receive enough phone calls at home, especially from annoying telemarketers. Why did I want everyone knowing where I was at all the time; besides, I might not want my kids to find me. When they call, they usually want money.

Can you imagine the puzzling look on Mr. Bell's face to see us driving or walking down the street with a phone in our hands? Nor would he understand our sitting across from one another in a restaurant, conversing with someone else on our cell phone, instead of our lunch companion.

Telephones can be a useful tool or a nuisance, depending on their use. I'm sure Mr. Bell had no concept of where his invention would lead. Nothing is more frustrating for me than to reach a business and hear a computerized voice giving me a series of options to choose from before I finally make contact with a real human. We've all been there.

Ironically, when you call the phone company, you get a series of options. However, I have to hit the pound key to listen to the options again. They don't always offer the option I need or by the time the mechanical voice gets to the end of the options, I have forgotten which one I need to select.

Imagine calling God and getting a busy signal. Or how about call waiting. Imagine calling heaven and getting the following options:

Press 1 to leave a prayer request.

Press 2 to speak to St. Peter who will decide if your prayer is really worth God's time.

Press 3 to ask why your prayer has not been answered.

Press 4 to speak to a customer service representative. Your call will be taken in the order that it was received. Your wait time will be approximately 10 years.

Press 5 if you need these options repeated.

Aren't we blessed that we have a direct line to God? We don't have to use any technology to communicate with Him on a daily basis. Through prayer and Bible study we can reach Him anytime, day or night. You won't get a busy signal or a list of options from which to choose.

Are you using your direct line to God? It's free. It's always available and He's waiting for your call.

It Isn't a Gift Until You Give it Away

"We have different gifts, according to the grace given us." Romans 12:6

When I was in elementary school—way back when—I dreaded math. I was not good at it.

Oh, I could do simple arithmetic, but when the problem became too complicated, forget it. That's why I would sit terrified that the teacher would call on me to go to the chalkboard and solve an equation before the class.

When I was in the fourth grade—that would have been in the 60s—the race was on to beat the Russians to the moon. This led to the teaching of "new math" or "space math" in many American schools.

I didn't care what they called it; it was still "way out there" for my math-impaired mind. My creative mind refuses to function with a formula.

While some people get high on solving algebraic equations, I can break out in hives if I am even exposed to a simple arithmetic problem.

A teaching friend of mine is an example of one who gets so excited when she is challenged with any type of mathematics problem that she almost bursts into a song and dance routine. One day we were discussing the benefits of being required to take college algebra.

Being mathematically-challenged, I could see no earthly reason why I, or anyone else who is handicapped like myself, should have to suffer through another semester of any type of math after graduation from high school.

It had been over 30 years since I had been forced to take college algebra. I told my friend, "If you placed an algebra test before me right now, held a gun to my head and told me

I had to pass the test, I'd have to say, 'Shoot me now, because I can't pass it.'"

My strengths are in reading and writing. I have loved the written word since I learned to read "See Dick and Jane." Give me a napkin and a writing utensil and I can fill the space with more than just directions. I love words.

According to my parents, my creative mind is not the only gift that God has given me.

When I was a child, my mother would grow tired of my incessant chattering. She would ask, "Carol, don't your jaws ever get tired."

Innocently, I'd answer, "No mama," to which she would reply, "Well, my ears sure do."

My Dad always said that I was vaccinated with a Victrola needle when I was born.

Until I read a chapter on applying your abilities in The Purpose Driven Life, I thought my motor mouth was a curse. In the book, Pastor Rick Warren says, "Your abilities are the natural talents you were born with. Some people have a natural ability with words: They came out of the womb talking!"

I confess. That's me.

We are all blessed with different gifts. As Pastor Warren says, "It would be a boring world if we were all plain vanilla."

Are you using your gifts to serve Him? A gift isn't a gift until you give it away.

Lost and Found

For the Son of Man came to seek and to save what was lost." Luke 19:10

Losing your car keys—or anything else for that matter—can be frustrating, especially if you are not in the habit of losing or misplacing items.

I recently misplaced my car keys. Fortunately, I had a spare set in my purse. However, my house key, safety deposit box key and my father's house key were on the lost key ring.

I have misplaced my keys before; however, they usually turn up after a quick search of my purse, house or car. This time, a search of my car and purse did not reveal the lost keys. I knew they were not in my house because I remembered putting them in my purse when I arrived at my destination in Tulsa.

I resigned myself to the fact that I had truly lost a set of keys for the first time in my life.

"Oh well," I thought, "I'll just get duplicates made tomorrow."

Later that evening I was searching my purse for a business card. You guessed it; I found my keys.

I thought I had looked in every nook and cranny and secret hiding place in that purse for my keys. But I had overlooked a small zippered pocket inside the bag—one of many.

We can lose many things: eyeglasses, jewelry, money, friends, loved ones and pets.

We can lose our hair, think we have lost our wits, and at times, we know we have lost our sense of humor. We want to lose weight and hope we don't lose our youth.

We can lose our patience .We can lose our way and we can lose hope. And some of us lose our sense of who we are.

We can also get lost in things, in success, in relationships, in trends and in self.

Many lost things can never be found nor replaced: lost time, lost opportunities, lost causes. If we were to take inventory of those things we have lost, we might feel an emptiness.

Helen Keller said, "Once I knew only darkness and stillness...my life was without past or future...but a little word from the fingers of another fell into my hand that clutched at emptiness, and my heart leaped to the rapture of living."

Like Helen Keller, we can embrace the rapture of living instead of allowing darkness and stillness to take over our lives by dwelling on what was lost. We can cling to the past and lose hope of a future or we can turn to the Lord.

He is the One who has stretched out his arms of hope. He is the only One who can lead us from emptiness to wholeness.

I once was lost but now I'm found. He saved a wretch like me.

He's searching for the lost. He will bring home the strays. There will be rejoicing.

Are you lost? Stand at the foot of the cross and seek the One who came to save.

Guess How Much He Loves You

"I pray that out of his glorious riches, he may strengthen you with power through his Spirit in your inner being, so that Christ may dwell in your hearts through faith. And I pray that you, being rooted and established in love may have power together with all the saints, to grasp how wide and long and high and deep is the love of Christ." Ephesians 3:16-18

Do you remember your first love?

Maybe you were in grade school. Maybe it was junior high. Even if you can't remember your age, you probably remember the feeling.

You wanted him or her to notice you. Maybe you picked a flower and pulled the petals off one-by-one and chanted, "He loves me. He loves me not. He loves me. He loves me not. He loves me. He loves me not . . . oh, just one more petal please. Disappointed, you threw the treacherous stem to the ground.

But then you grew up—hopefully—to realize that love can't be measured by the number of petals on a flower.

I can remember when my sons were young. We would play a game. They would ask me, "Mama, how much do you love us?"

I would hold my hands about two feet apart and say, "This is how much I love you."

"Is that all?"

I'd laugh and move my hands farther apart. Again, they would ask, "Is that all, Mama?"

This game would continue until my arms would stretch as far as they could. Then, I would reply. "My love for you can't be measured."

34

I now have two grandbabies. I think the sweetest words I have ever heard are, "I love you Nana."

I recently bought my granddaughter the classic book "Guess How Much I Love You?"

The story's plot revolves around Little Nutbrown Hare asking Big Nutbrown Hare, "Guess how much I love you?" to which he replies, "Oh, I don't think I could guess that."

As the little hare uses different ways to show how much he loves Big Nutbrown Hare, the older rabbit always replies with a demonstration of his own love. By the last page, we find out that the little hare's love for the bigger hare is very hard to measure.

At the end of the story, the little hare looks out into the dark night and says, "I love you right up to the moon," to which the big hare replies, "That is very, very far."

As the little rabbit drifts off to sleep, Big Nutbrown Hare leans over and kisses him good night. His final words are, "I love you right up to the moon—and back."

How much can you love someone? We don't have to guess how much we are loved by God. We can fall asleep at night secure that His love for us is beyond measure.

Can you grasp how wide and long and high and deep is the love of Christ? Look at the cross. See his outstretched arms. Guess how much He loves you.

Getting Dirty for the Lord

"He is like a well-watered plant in the sunshine, spreading its shoots over the garden." JOB 8:16

As a child, I loved playing in the dirt. I still do.

I was working in my flower beds recently doing some major overhauling when a neighbor came home from work. He hollered across the street at me, "What are you doing?"

Sitting in the dirt because my knees were hurting, I hollered back, "I'm making mud pies. Do you want one?"

Laughing, he replied, "Are you reliving your childhood?"

"Yes," I said and continued getting my hands deep into the soil. I love the feel of the cool dirt on my skin; most of the time, you won't find me wearing gardening gloves.

When other neighbors—who are out walking their dogs—see me on my knees in the dirt, they often comment, "You sure are working hard."

For me, it is not work but a joy to spend that time enjoying God's wonders. You never know what you will unearth when you turn over a spade of dirt—a chubby white grub or a slimy brown fishing worm.

A friend, who had been on vacation—not away from home but from a busy time at work—recently emailed me. She had spent her days off, not on a sandy beach somewhere, but digging in the dirt and praying.

She said, "It's amazing how much clutter we build up in our hearts and minds over days, weeks and even years of working and living. Digging in the dirt reminds me of how basic we really are."

Her insight made me realize why working in the soil is healing.

Like most humans, we seek our creature comforts. We worry too much about what we are going to eat, how we are going to pay the bills, and how we can afford the desires of our hearts.

But when we spend time working the soil, pulling out the weeds, planting seeds and watering our plants, we are also feeding and nurturing our spiritual selves.

Four years ago, I was going through some difficult times. I spent many hours in my flower beds. Although my thoughts were troubled when I first struck the dry dirt with my shovel, my heart, my mind and my spirit refused to remain in turmoil with each weed that was removed and with each flower that was tenderly rooted into the ground.

Like the flowers that grow in our gardens, we can nurture our spiritual selves or we can let the weeds of despair choke out life's joys. We have an option to mature through spiritual growth, but like the plants in our garden, we must feed and water our soul if we want to produce fruit.

Producing fruit requires time and patience. But the results are worth the effort—even if we get our hands dirty in the process.

Are you getting your hands dirty for the Lord? Feed your mind, heart and spirit. Spread your roots and bloom.

Honk if You Love Peace and Quiet

"Be still, and know that I am God." Psalm 46:10

Honk if you love peace and quiet.

When I saw this sign posted outside a local business, my first inclination was to honk. Instead, while the traffic light was red, I grabbed the notebook I always carry with me. I scribbled down the sign's message but not before the driver in the car behind me honked.

I smiled. Another driver agreed with me. He loved peace and quiet too.

When I heard another long, insistent honk, I glanced in my rearview mirror. The driver was not smiling. I glanced at the traffic light. It was green.

I tossed my notebook in the passenger seat and pressed the accelerator. Evidently not everyone likes peace and quiet.

Peace and quiet in today's world is sometimes hard to find. It's called noise pollution. Noise is one of the most prevalent pollutants today.

We are constantly bombarded with noises from every direction: road traffic, jet planes, garbage trucks, trains, construction equipment, lawn mowers, leaf blowers, car alarms, television, cell phones and boom boxes that threaten to vibrate you off the planet. These are just a few of the audible polluters that litter the air.

Noise negatively affects our health and well-being. Noise related problems include hearing loss, stress, high blood pressure, sleep loss, distraction and lost productivity. Overall, the cacophony of sounds causes a general reduction in the quality of life and opportunities for tranquility.

The old saying "silence is golden" is true. How often in our external world do we crave the sound of silence?

Many equate quietness with emptiness and solitude with loneliness. Many are afraid to be alone with the silence. They keep the television or radio on—just for company. Many cannot function without this background noise.

Sometimes we forget the purpose that silence serves. I welcome the silence that a quiet time brings. It is a priority with me because it is in the silence that I can most clearly hear God's voice.

In our modern world, it requires a creative effort to find that time and space where we can carve out our own silent time. When we learn the power that quiet time can have in our lives, we crave more. Silence is therapeutic—a pause that refreshes.

Without silence, without the quiet, we cannot appreciate who we are as a child of God. Without the background babble in our daily lives, we can renew our spirits.

Try going for a walk, a run or a bike ride. Leave the headphones behind. Tune into nature's music. When was the last time you stopped to hear the birds sing or the wind blowing through the branches of a tree? Have you heard the waves lapping against the shore lately or the sound of wind chimes rustled by a quiet breeze?

What do you hear when you stop to listen? Silence. Embrace it. It gives you time to reflect and to pray.

When was the last time you nurtured your spirit? Be still and know the Lord.

Following God's Road Map

"Thomas said to him, 'Lord, we do not know where you are going; how can we know the way?' Jesus said to him, 'I am the way, and the truth, and the life; no one comes to the Father, but by me. If you had known me, you would have known my Father also; henceforth you know him and have seen him.'" John 14:5-7

Have you ever found yourself lost in an unfamiliar city? I have.

I have had to stop and ask for directions. Even then I sometimes still end up lost.

Don't ask me for directions unless you are familiar with local landmarks? I might tell you to go approximately ten miles, then turn left when you see Arby's on the corner. Hang a right at the next stoplight and look for a green truck parked in the drive of a red brick house on the left side of the road. Confusing? Not to me...unless the green truck has moved.

I am confused, however, if someone gives me directions to follow and tells me to head north when I reach the intersection of 3rd and Main. Is that right or left?

I am one of the directionally challenged. I am good at plotting my route if I am headed for a new destination. I can read the map, follow signs, and pray that there is no major road construction that messes up my carefully planned route. If there is, I can easily get lost if there are no detour signs.

On a group road trip, I have no trouble getting us to our destination if I have a navigator in the vehicle that is good at reading a map and giving me instructions. Even in a large city, I can whiz in and out of traffic and make the correct exit—most of the time—with the help of friends.

Not bad for a woman who put off getting her driver's license for a year after she was eligible because she was afraid to parallel park. I still avoid parallel parking.

Fear and a lack of direction in our lives can paralyze us. We can become so afraid of making a mistake or of taking a wrong turn, that we don't see the doors of opportunity to learn, to grow and to become the person that God created us to be.

Some of us are too proud to ask for directions and end up lost on a road to nowhere. We spend our lives searching for the right path but never find it.

We ignore signs of trouble and forget to stop along the way to seek help. When we come to a roadblock, instead of slowing down, some of us speed ahead ignoring the warning signs.

The best road map for life is God's word. When He is in the driver's seat, He will lead you safely through the detours and the potholes to arrive safely at your final destination.

Do you trust His directions? God not only knows where He is taking you, He knows how to get you there.

Are we Really Free?

"But whenever anyone turns to the Lord, the veil is taken away. Now the Lord is the Spirit, and where the Spirit of the Lord is, there is freedom." 2 Corinthians 3:16-17

I was comparing the nutritional values on the back of different cereal boxes recently when an older gentleman said, "I can't believe how many different cereals there are today. It's hard to decide which one to buy when there are so many choices."

I had to agree with him. But it's not just cereal. Stroll down the bread aisle and you won't just find white and wheat anymore. Let's see, there's whole wheat, multi-grain, whole grain, honey wheat—now there's even whole grain white—or something like that. It's confusing.

Each day we are faced with choices. Some choices are insignificant while others determine our future. If we choose to eat a doughnut instead of a healthy bowl of oatmeal for breakfast, it may seem unimportant at that moment. Continue to make that choice every day and you'll soon be wearing those doughnuts on your hips and thighs and your cholesterol will be off the charts.

Freedom is the capacity to exercise choice but if we are not careful, we can become slaves to our desires, slaves to bitterness, slaves to hatred and slaves to our pride. Any choice that keeps us from being the person that God created us to be keeps us in bondage.

For many years, I was a slave to other people's opinions of me. I became a people pleaser instead of doing those things that I knew pleased God. I could not become the person He wanted me to be because I wasn't seeking His guidance. Instead, I was seeking the approval of man.

God empowers us to make the right choices but fear of rejection or of others' disapproval often leads us to compromise what we believe or what we know in our hearts is right.

Being bombarded daily by media messages that tell us we must look and act a certain way does not help. We get a distorted image of ourselves because we think we don't measure up and we become slaves to society's definition of freedom. True freedom is realizing that a daily walk with the Lord is all we need to break the chains of oppression.

Recently, I was reading a devotional by noted pastor and author, Charles Stanley, whose article posed the question, "Are you free?" In America we would say, "Yes," based on the fact that we can go almost anywhere we choose and do what we like without anyone interfering.

Man's definition of freedom and God's definition, however, are not the same. While the constitution grants us many rights as citizens of the United States, true freedom is won within the boundaries of God's word.

Scripture reveals to us how to release those chains that hold us hostage. If we allow our human natures to be in control, then we are stepping outside the boundaries and we are not free.

Will you choose the path that leads to true freedom? Choose God.

And That Has Made All the Difference

"Here I am! I stand at the door and knock. If anyone hears my voice and opens the door, I will come in and eat with him, and he with me." Revelation 3:20

I grew up attending a small church that was only a block from where my sister and I grew up. We walked to Sunday school each week.

Eventually I drifted away from the church. And though I have always believed in God, I didn't know Him.

We can attend church every time the doors are open. We can listen to the sermon, sing hymns of praise, participate in church activities and still walk out the door without knowing the Lord personally.

About six years ago, I realized that something was missing in my life. I didn't know what it was. I just felt this gnawing emptiness inside that nothing could ease.

Shopping for clothes, shoes, purses and jewelry gave me a temporary high. Staying busy to occupy every waking moment didn't fill that hole. Escaping through reading one fiction book after another provided no relief. Working harder to earn more money couldn't fill me up. Neither could the various dating relationships I had.

Nothing could fill that void in my heart except a personal relationship with my savior. He continued to patiently knock at the door until I opened it and let Him in. And that has made all the difference.

God's patience with me has helped me to be more patient with those around me. His acceptance of me—faults and all—has made me less critical of others. His willingness to forgive me has led me to forgive those who have hurt me. By His grace, I am a new person.

I sometimes refer to myself as the "old Carol" and the "new Carol" when talking about the change in me. Those who know me best have seen the transformation.

Another word for transformation is adaptation. The definition of adaptation "is the acquisition of modifications in an organism that enable it to adjust to life in a new environment."

I have willingly allowed the Lord to transform me so that I can adjust to life in a new environment—an environment of love and acceptance because He first loved and accepted the person I was and who I have become through a personal relationship with Him.

I am still working—with His help—on becoming the woman He created me to be. I am a work-in-progress like the pieces of a puzzle that must patiently be fitted together to form a picture.

Many people have the pre-conceived idea that when you accept the Lord into your life, all of your troubles will magically disappear. Actually, my disappointments, my heartaches and serious illnesses increased—but so did my faith.

When I began to feel unfulfilled and empty, I think Jesus was knocking louder. His knock was more urgent. He was preparing me for what was to come.

I'm so thankful that He kept knocking—so blessed that He didn't give up on me.

Do you hear Him knocking at your door? Open it. Let Him in.

A Matter of Duty

"Now all has been heard; here is the conclusion of the matter: Fear God and keep his commandments, for this is the whole duty of man." Ecclesiastes 12:13

It was only $6.30.

It would have put about two gallons of gas in my vehicle—depending on the whim of whomever decides to raise or lower gas prices on any given day. But it wasn't my money.

Oh, I had it in my possession. It was weighing down my billfold. More precisely, it was weighing on my heart.

I was in a hurry—who isn't these days? I had paid for some photos at a local store and stuffed the change in my billfold without thinking. I was leaving town for the weekend and I couldn't wait to get to the lake where I craved solitary time with the Lord.

I was probably five minutes out of town when I realized that I had received too much change. As I recalled the exchange with the young photo clerk, I remembered him counting out my money. It suddenly dawned on me what he had done.

Instead of giving me the correct change out of a $10 bill, he had actually given me the amount I owed for the photos. Neither one of us had caught the mistake. Both of us probably had our minds on weekend plans. I certainly did.

It was five days later before I found the time to return to the store. I asked to speak to the manager. When I told him my story, he checked the records and confirmed that the register had been $6.30 short that day. I opened my billfold and counted out six $1 bills and 30 cents in change.

Two other store employees, who witnessed our conversation, were amazed that I had returned to correct the mistake. One said, "Most people wouldn't have bothered."

In the past, I didn't bother. I figured it was the store's loss and my gain when I was given too much change at the time of a purchase. I didn't feel convicted to fix the oversight.

But that was before I knew my savior personally. When you enter into a relationship with the Lord, your whole outlook changes. You come to a place within yourself where you know that you have to please Him. Nothing else matters.

I was listening to one of my favorite TV pastors the other day. One of the things she mentioned was our duty to please the Lord. Duty? I had never thought of it as a duty.

I turned to my dictionary where I looked up the definition of "duty" and its synonyms. Duty means responsibility. Other words that mean the same include assignment, commission, commitment, mission, obligation, service, task and undertaking.

We have a responsibility to God. You may consider it mere pocket change. He sees it as your mission to live your life for Him.

Are you living out your life for Him? It's your duty, you know.

Don't Save the Good Stuff

He said to them, "Therefore every teacher of the law who has been instructed about the kingdom of heaven is like the owner of a house who brings out of his storeroom new treasures as well as old. Matthew 13:52

I opened the cabinet door where I keep my drinking glasses. The cupboard was almost empty. Two glasses stared from the shelf.

I usually have plenty of containers from which to drink. My dishwasher was full of dirty ones; I had forgotten to start the machine the night before. The sink was also overflowing because when it's hot outside, I drink more.

I scrutinized the pair of lonely drinking utensils. One was a tall iced tea glass while the other was a long-stemmed piece that I saved for special occasions. You have to understand that I am not fussy about my dishes. My kitchen cabinets are a hodge podge of glassware with only one set of four that matches.

Although I was preparing to pour a glass of iced tea, I didn't reach for the tall glass; instead, I decided to use the long-stemmed one. I didn't have a specific reason for grabbing it off the shelf that morning. I just felt compelled to use it after two conversations I had recently.

The first exchange was with a friend who had been cleaning out her kitchen drawers and cabinets. She had many mismatched pieces of everyday eating utensils. She didn't mind; sometimes—with her large family of six children and 13 grandbabies—things have a habit of disappearing over time. Spoons make great digging tools for sandboxes or for mixing up mud pies.

Sharon had decided to get rid of all the mismatched utensils and use the good silverware that had belonged to her mother-in-law. After all, she said, it rarely gets used. It is removed from its storage container, polished for special family gatherings and returned to hiding until the next time.

My other friend, Teresa, was relating a story to me about the special relationship between her father and her son. Her father is now deceased but she recalled how the pair would use the long-stemmed crystal glasses to drink their orange juice—only when Teresa's mother was not around.

I have visited with cancer survivors and others who have faced serious medical conditions. Most have come to realize the importance of not saving the "good" stuff to celebrate an occasion. I, too, came to this realization when I was diagnosed with cancer four years ago. Why let those beautiful pieces gather dust while they are hiding behind closed cabinet doors, packed away in a chest or stuffed in a drawer?

People are like that too. God wants us to use our "good" stuff everyday to shine for Him. They are His gift to us. If we only bring those qualities out for special occasions, they will lose their luster and benefit no one.

Are your "good" qualities hidden away? Search your heart. Seek the Lord. Share the "good" stuff everyday.

The Power of a Simple Hug

"My command is this: Love each other as I have loved you." John 15:12

I didn't know her but I felt led to give her a hug. She needed one and so did I.

It was a hectic day. In my rush to get everything done, I decided to stop by a small, local store to pick up a birthday card for my grandson. Choosing convenience that day was a God-sent moment for me and for the woman I encountered stocking shelves. Her wrinkles and grey hair were a testimony to having lived a full life.

Our paths crossed that day in the crowded aisle where I was trying to navigate my way through a maze of boxes waiting to be unpacked. She asked me if I needed help. Smiling, I replied, "No, I found what I came for: a birthday card for my grandson."

Our conversation turned to grandkids. She had none of her own. In fact, she and her husband of more than 50 years had no children.

But her eyes lit up when she talked about the comfort that a neighbor's child brought to her ailing husband. He was suffering from a multitude of health problems. Her eyes filled with tears as she talked about her spouse. She was still working to help support them.

My arms enfolded her in a hug. She was a stranger to me but that brief encounter lifted both of our spirits.

Academic studies have found that hugging, handholding and other forms of TLC are good for our health. I recall reading a story about twin girls born prematurely. Doctors didn't expect the smaller girl to live.

However, a nurse didn't give up hope. She placed the sisters together in one incubator. The photo that accompanied the story revealed the miracle that a hug can bring. The stronger of the twins had placed her arm around her sibling. As they slept together in their little cocoon, something happened. The weaker of the two grew stronger. She survived.

Earlier this month, a deadly Hezbollah attack in northern Israel left two Israeli brothers dead. Their surviving brother wanted his brothers' eyes donated to help someone in need. A long list of patients included an Arab who was blind in one eye and had nearly lost vision in the other.

With permission from the Israeli, the Arab received one of the eyes. When the Arab learned that a Jewish man was the donor, he was confused. After all, there is a war between Israelis and Arabs and the Arab had received the cornea of a Jewish man killed by an Arab missile.

After the successful surgery, the Arab wanted to meet his benefactor. When the two met, they exchanged phone numbers and a hug, bringing hope in a war zone.

The television anchor's comment, "So much meaning in a hug," was a reminder to me that Jesus has asked us to love others as He has loved us.

Loving others as our Lord loves us binds us together in perfect unity. It's powerful. Can you feel it?

A Day Hemmed in Prayer

"Is any one of you in trouble? He should pray. Is anyone happy? Let him sing songs of praise." James 5:13

Like many young children, my granddaughter will not go to sleep without her favorite "blankie." Its softness and a picture of Winnie the Pooh provide security to a child who has yet to understand the ultimate comforter.

I, too, had need for a security blanket when I was younger. Buried inside my cedar chest is a handmade baby quilt that my grandmother made over 50 years ago. In each of the twelve blocks is a lamb. The hand-sewn details are intricate.

The time that my grandmother put into stitching the quilt for me is evidence of her love before I was ever born. Stains now grace the blanket and the edges are frayed, a testimony of my attachment to this childhood comfort.

Throughout our lives we become attached to things or relationships that we think are necessary to our wellbeing and happiness. Then something happens, causing us to re-evaluate their importance.

We struggle, hanging on even when it is no longer what we need or what God wants for our life. In our desire to keep things the way they are, our lives sometimes unravel because we cling too tightly to the status quo.

When we are attached to yesterday, we can't move forward. When we are afraid of change, we become stagnant. Look up the definition of stagnant and you'll find: motionless, dormant, idle, inactive, inert, lifeless, sluggish, stale, stationary, still and unmoving.

The opposite of stagnant is active and flowing. How can we move out of our comfort zone with confidence so that God can do a good work in us?

We can follow Jesus' example. He spent time alone in the wilderness each morning in prayer. During quiet time with the Lord, we become energized and gain a new perspective if we listen for His voice.

The Lord's voice is the reassurance that we need to move forward, letting go of our "security blankets" and stepping out in faith. It is the only sustenance we need to fill our lives with confidence that we are a child of God.

As a child, I found solace in my baby blanket. As an adult, I find peace from knowing the Lord.

I start each morning with prayer but also turn to Him throughout my day in praise and thanksgiving. I strive to stay God-centered by putting Him in the middle of my day as well as at the beginning and at the end.

Christians often wonder: "How can I spend all of my time in prayer?" I used to ask the same question. You don't have to spend every minute in prayer but you can have an ongoing conversation with Him. When your focus is on serving Him, you can pray any time, even while talking with others.

Did you know God is always present, always listening and always ready to answer? When you hem your day in prayer, it never unravels.

It's Not About You

"Rather, clothe yourselves with the Lord Jesus Christ, and do not think about how to gratify the desires of the sinful nature." Romans 13:14

"It's mine."

If you've ever watched two children playing together, you've probably heard those words before. Like most two-year-olds, my granddaughter has to learn the concept of sharing with her younger brother.

She's learning. Sometimes she conveniently forgets. Recently, she took a toy away from her brother and told her parents: "Look, Bubba is sharing."

Sharing does not come naturally to humans. When we are born, our needs are focused on "what's in it for me?" When we come out of the womb, we're crying. We're hungry. We're tired. We're scared.

Our needs are simple. Feed me. Change me. Hold me. Comfort me. As we grow, our needs change but they are still basic. We not only need food to sustain our bodies but we need love to help us thrive.

Somewhere in the growing process though, we confuse need and want because we are born selfish. We have to learn selflessness. Letting go of self is not an easy process. It requires daily effort, especially in our "me first" society.

The advertising and marketing world reinforces that "It's all about me" mentality. Look at some of the slogans: "Because I'm worth it." "Have it your way." "It's everywhere you want to be." "When you got it, flaunt it." "Double your pleasure, double your fun."

When the focus is on our pleasure and having our way, we miss God's best for our lives. One of my favorite advertising slogans is "Reach out and touch someone."

As I was leaving church one morning last fall, I met a woman struggling to open the heavy glass door. Her right arm was in a sling. Although she was wearing a turban, it didn't dawn on me that she was battling cancer. I saw her struggle and assumed she had a broken arm. I rushed to open the door for her. After she thanked me, I inquired about her arm. She told me of her battle with cancer and the resulting problems with lymphedema or arm swelling.

Our conversation has led to a close friendship because I am a cancer survivor too. I am blessed because mine was diagnosed early. I did not need chemo or radiation. My friend was not so fortunate.

Patti, however, doesn't feel sorry for herself. Her attitude toward life is a blessing to me as well as to others. In fact, this tiny woman is also dealing with her husband's health problems. She is focused, not on self, but on helping others even though she spends most of her days at the doctor's office or visiting her husband who is confined to a rehab center.

Caught up in self, we forget our purpose. Just as Jesus humbled himself to wash the feet of his disciples, so must we humble ourselves to serve others.

Are you self-centered or other-centered? Remember, it's not about you.

God Has a Sense of Humor

"But the Lord laughs at the wicked for He knows their day is coming." Psalms 37:13

I'm sure God has a sense of humor.

Some may disagree but I'm not about to write a thesis to prove my point. I'm merely sharing my thoughts on this subject.

Raised to believe in a stern figure that was going to strike me dead if I didn't follow the rules, I never considered that humor is one of God's character traits. The Bible says that God created man in His image and since most of us have a sense of humor that must mean that God does too.

Besides sharing in each other's grief, what trait can bring two people closer together? I believe it's humor.

Humor comes in many forms: sarcasm, exaggeration, puns, wordplays, riddles, jokes, irony, wit, slapstick, farce, caricatures and parody. While there are differences in these types of humor, they have one thing in common: they have the ability to make us laugh, smile or chuckle.

Now if we can share a good belly laugh and it brings us closer, what makes us think that God doesn't want that same closeness? Besides, I think it makes Him more approachable.

I was reading an essay titled "Does the God of the Bible laugh?" The writer pointed out something I have always wondered about: the creation of some of the oddest-looking creatures I have ever seen. Take, for example, the porcupine, the armadillo and the anteater, not to mention the duck-billed platypus. What was God thinking when He created these funny-looking animals?

God also had to have a sense of humor to create human beings in the first place. I'm sure that when we keep repeating the same mistakes over and over, He laughs at the futility of our efforts. Read the Bible from cover to cover and you'll find that humankind hasn't changed.

I like to think that God created humor as a survival tool. Rabbi and humorist Moshe Waldoks once said, "A sense of humor can help you overlook the unattractive, tolerate the unpleasant, cope with the unexpected, and smile through the unbearable."

Having a sense of humor can get us through many trials in life. Humor helped me keep my life in perspective when I was facing cancer. In fact, the origin of the term derives from the humoral medicine of the ancient Greeks, which stated that a mix of fluids known as humours controlled human health and emotion.

I was having lunch with a married couple last week. My friend, Charlie, has to be married to one of the funniest men I know. He had us laughing hysterically at his jokes and antics. I told my friend, "When a man can make you laugh, he's worth his weight in gold."

In that case, said her husband, "I'm worth a lot."

I believe that God wants us to be happy. He wants us to enjoy life.

If God didn't have a sense of humor, why did He create man with a funny bone? Just hit your elbow on something and you'll know what I mean.

It's More than Etiquette

"Yet he has not left himself without testimony: He has shown kindness by giving you rain from heaven and crops in their seasons; he provides you with plenty of food and fills your hearts with joy." ACTS 14:17

"What wisdom can you find that is greater than kindness?"

These words on a bumper sticker caught my attention recently. I delight in stickers that have something positive to say because they speak loudly about the vehicle owner.

Is kindness in short supply these days? I guess it depends on where you live. I was reminded of this when a girl in her late teens held the door open for me as I was leaving a doctor's office recently. She not only stepped back to allow me to exit first but she told me "to have a good afternoon."

Holding open the door for another person, regardless of his or her age or gender, is a common courtesy. Yet many adults don't practice this kindness.

So what's our excuse for not showing others the kindness they deserve? Are we too busy? Too filled with our own self-importance that we can't see another human being in need? Too afraid to reach out to a stranger?

A recent article about modern manners in an area newspaper caught my attention for two reasons. I find human behavior fascinating, and a friend of mine who teaches etiquette classes, was interviewed for the story.

The first time I met Jana and had lunch with her, I was afraid of committing a dining faux pas. I was glad we were eating at a sandwich shop where I didn't have to worry about which fork to use.

After we became friends, I told her how I had squirmed through that first meeting, hoping that she wasn't grading me on my table manners. She laughed and said, "I would never do that."

Since Jana and I are both country girls, I figured that drying my hands on my jeans was acceptable after we became friends—at least in some social settings. What is not acceptable to God, however, is our lack of kindness to others.

Although my friend teaches social and business protocol, including when it is appropriate to open doors for female co-workers, she says, "It's okay to open doors for others, too. Kindness is kindness, no matter what the setting."

However, it's not just about opening doors for others. Kind gestures require us to be aware of others around us who need kind words of encouragement. As Mother Teresa once said, "Kind words can be short and easy to speak, but their echoes are truly endless."

Opportunities present themselves each day for us to show we care. Smiling at a stranger is another way. When you acknowledge another human being, you are saying, "I think you are important."

As the Lord has rained down his goodness on us, let us extend that hand to others.

Is your hand clenched in selfishness or is it reaching out to others? You can't open the door of kindness if your heart is locked.

Time to Go Fishing

"Come, follow me," Jesus said, "and I will make you fishers of men." Matthew 4:19

"Gone fishing."

If you remember the old Andy Griffith series, you can probably recall that sign posted on the door of Floyd's barbershop door when he was closed. It brings back fond memories of simpler times.

October might seem like a strange time to talk about fishing but as I was walking near a local lake recently, I saw several people who were taking advantage of the warm weather to cast their lines in the water. As I walked around the lake, I recalled my own childhood experiences with fishing.

I was never really too keen on the idea. I liked eating the fish but I was squeamish about sticking a hook through the worm. I didn't mind holding the squirmy critter. I just hated to hurt them.

I grew up in Louisiana where fishing was a cinch. We grabbed a cane pole, a cork bobber and a Styrofoam container of worms and headed to the nearest bayou. All we had to worry about on those lazy summer afternoons were water moccasins.

On more than one occasion, however, my dad would find my nose in a library book and my bobber bobbing. He'd have to holler, "Carol, you've got one."

When my youngest son was around 10, I fixed several trout that my sister and her husband had caught on a fishing trip to Missouri. When she gave them to me, they were frozen. When I thawed the package to prepare them, I found that the heads were intact.

Because I had never prepared trout, I called my sister for cooking instructions. I carefully followed her guidelines for baking the fish whole.

However, when I placed the dish on the table, my youngest son, who is a picky eater, said, "Okay, mom, what's for supper."

I replied, "You're looking at it," to which he exclaimed, "I'm not eating anything that is staring at me."

I quickly solved the problem. I grabbed a large chopping knife and dismembered the poor thing—not my son, the fish. My son still didn't eat too much of that trout.

My grandchildren have been learning how to fish. My granddaughter, who is almost three, is already telling fish stories about the big one that got away. With my grandson, Brennan, you just have to make sure he doesn't eat the worms.

One of my girlfriends has a husband who likes to fish in bass tournaments. He will drive out-of-state to participate in these contests. When I asked him recently if he had brought any home to eat, he replied, "No, we throw them back."

Evidently, I don't understand the basics of bass fishing. To me, if you catch a fish and it's big enough to eat, you should clean it and slap it in the frying pan.

As God's children, we are called to become fishers of men. No cane pole or bait is required. You just need a heart for the Lord.

Are you fishing for men? People need to hear the good news.

Called to Make a Difference

"Then the King will say, 'I'm telling the solemn truth: Whenever you did one of these things to someone overlooked or ignored, that was me—you did it to me."Matthew 25:40 (The Message)

During my college years, I was actively involved in campus activities, including student government, the college newspaper and various other organizations.

When eighteen-year-olds were given the right to vote in the early 70s, my roommate and I became involved in politics. We attended political rallies and even traveled off-campus for some events. We were vocal but we didn't feel like our voices were being heard.

I have discovered, however, that making a difference in the world doesn't mean you have to raise your voice. We can whisper and still be heard.

Recently, I had the opportunity to interview area volunteers involved with different programs for a newspaper feature. These volunteers give, not because they have time, but because they have heart. Through their selfless actions, lives are changed.

A young man who is still touching lives today died three weeks before his fourteenth birthday on June 22, 2004. Mattie Stepanek made an impression on people around the world because his message of hope and peace reached individuals of all ages, genders, races, nationalities, faiths, abilities and vocations.

Mattie began writing poetry at age three to express his feelings about his life-threatening illness. The rare form of muscular dystrophy had already taken the lives of his three siblings. His mother, Jeni Stepanek, who survives, suffers from a milder version.

Mattie's poetry has been published in seven books. The latest, "Just Peace: A Message of Hope," was released by his mother this year. It is the final collection and his legacy of hope and peace to the world.

During his short lifetime, Mattie chose to live with hope. He required a ventilator and a wheelchair but they did not hold him back. When he was born, the doctors didn't think he'd live one day, but he did. Then the medical community didn't think he would survive beyond a year, but he did. As young Mattie said, "I think I'm here for a reason."

During his journey through life, Mattie made many friends, appeared on many well-known talk shows, and met people in public life who were also inspired by this philosophical, upbeat and insightful youngster, including Jimmy Carter and Oprah Winfrey.

Mattie knew that each day he lived was a gift, and he made the most of it. He credited his strength to God and his mom, and from the people who become part of his circle of life.

Mattie once said, "People tell me I inspire them. And that inspires me. It's a beautiful circle, and we all go around together, with and for each other. What a gift."

Mattie Stepanek, who made a difference during his short time on earth, was truly a gift from God. All of us are called to make a difference while we are here.

What is God calling you to do? Hear His whisper. Make a difference.

The Greatest Gift of All

"For God so loved the world that he gave his one and only Son, that whoever believes in him shall not perish but have eternal life." John 3:16

Can you imagine what it must have been like on that cold, starry night in Bethlehem? Mary and Joseph alone, except for the animals whose home they had invaded in preparation for the birth of their child.

No modern-day birthing room or a luxury hotel. No heat. No electricity. No running water. No bed to rest their weary bodies as they awaited the birth of their child. No place for a small babe except a feeding trough for His cradle. However, it was from these humble beginnings that God gave us the greatest gift of all.

Christmas is a time to remember that gift which, in reality, would become a sacrifice. With the advertising blitz and the glittery glitz of today's holiday season, how can we relate to that night over 2,000 years ago?

We must first remember the tiny package that was delivered into His mother's arms and wrapped in swaddling clothes. Good things do come in small packages.

In spite of all the modern-day toys with their bells and whistles, most children are content to play with the wrapping paper and bows. I have observed not only my sons' but also my grandchildren's fascination with simple things: a cardboard box, pots and pans, a wooden spoon or an empty paper towel tube.

I can recall a discarded refrigerator box that my two sons confiscated. Over several months, the cardboard metamorphosed from a tunnel to a fort and into a variety of other little boys' playthings, before the pieces that remained were tossed in the trash.

I have listened to my parents tell stories of growing up during the Depression. My grandparents used their imagination to create toys from items that we would probably throw away in our wasteful society today.

A toy tractor made from a wooden spool, a sliver of soap, matches and a rubber band provided hours of fun for my father and his brothers who would race their new vehicles on the smooth wooden floors of their parents' home. Their homemade treasures were created from improvised items by parents who had to "make-do" when life was really less complicated.

Parents didn't have to worry about standing in long lines to fight for their chance to purchase a popular novelty item, stay up all night on Christmas Eve to assemble a toy or race at the last minute to purchase batteries for a gift that would not walk or talk without them.

Mary and Joseph had to "make-do" in their circumstances. But it was from these humble beginnings that God gave us His Son, the greatest gift of all.

As we prepare to celebrate Christmas, avoid being consumed by the glamour of the season. Instead, remember that tiny baby who was born in simple surroundings.

What does this season mean to you? When you have received the greatest gift of all, the others pale in comparison.

Forgiveness is a Choice

"For if you forgive men when they sin against you, your heavenly Father will also forgive you." Matthew 6:14

As legend goes, a now-famous feud began with a dispute over the ownership of a hog. The feud escalated and lives were lost on both sides.

The battle between the Hatfields and McCoys continued for 12 years until they agreed to disagree. But it wasn't until June 14, 2003, that descendants of both sides signed a truce, though the conflict had ended a century earlier.

Lewis B. Smedes, author and professor, once said, "If we wait too long to forgive, our rage settles in and claims squatter's rights to our souls."

Four months before the last of my Dad's three brothers succumbed to cancer, I wanted my father to reconcile with him. A family dispute five years earlier had left my Dad bitter and he had refused to talk to my Uncle Joe ever since.

But my uncle was dying. I knew Dad would regret it if he did not make peace with the past. Before my uncle's death, he and my father spent many hours together talking about their childhood, among other things. They never mentioned the rift but my father was grateful for the nudge I gave him to move toward forgiveness.

Numerous scientific studies tout the benefits to our health when we forgive those who have wronged us. Chronic anger and stress are almost unavoidable consequences of an unwillingness to forgive. Both are toxic to our physical and emotional health.

Just before Christmas last year, I was led to purchase a book for a friend who was bitter about his wife's betrayal and their subsequent divorce.

As I browsed through the various books at a Christian bookstore, I asked the owner for suggestions, explaining the reason for my search. I wanted to find a book for my friend that would help him to begin the journey to freedom and eventual healing.

When she made the following statement, I asked her to write it down: "When I forgave, I set a prisoner free. Then I realized the prisoner was me."

Before I mailed the book to my friend, I wrote those words, along with the following scripture from Matthew 6:14, on the inside cover: "For if you forgive men when they sin against you, your heavenly Father will also forgive you."

Author Catherine Ponder once said, "When you hold resentment toward another, you are bound to that person or condition by an emotional link that is stronger than steel. Forgiveness is the only way to dissolve that link and get free."

We, as followers of Christ, are a forgiven people but the Bible also makes it clear that we are to be a forgiving people. Forgiving someone who has wronged us is not easy but it is the only way we can be free to be the person that God intends us to be.

Whom do you need to forgive? Forgiveness is a choice and a gift we give to ourselves.

My Cup is Overflowing

". . . give thanks in all circumstances, for this is God's will for you in Christ Jesus." 1 Thessalonians 5:18

My first reaction was anger. I wanted to get my hands on that crazy driver in the Lexus and choke him.

After the initial shock had worn off, I realized how close I had come to being involved in a nasty accident. Anger immediately gave way to thanks.

Giving thanks is not always our first reaction in a situation, especially when we focus on what we don't have and what could have happened. I took a different route that day. If I had not done so, the car that almost sideswiped me might have hit someone else.

I chose not to dwell on the anger I felt at the carelessness of the other person. Instead, I lifted up my voice and said, "Thank you, God."

If you had been a passenger in my car, you would have witnessed a miracle. If my window had been rolled down, I could have reached out and touched the shiny black metal of the other vehicle. Who knows what other blessings have come from this incident?

If you have heard the stories of individuals who should have been at the Twin Towers on September 11, 2001, you know that God's hand was on each one. A pen pal of mine who lives in Canada had an office at the World Trade Center. He would have been there the morning of the attack if he had not gone to traffic court for a speeding ticket. Everyone who worked in the area of his office died that day.

We can easily give thanks for the times we have survived major trials in life. But what about the small, everyday things we take for granted?

If you could get out of bed by yourself this morning, give thanks. Even if you have aches and pains that make it difficult for you to rise, be thankful for the pain. You're still alive.

The Bible tells us in 1Thessalonians 5:18, *"give thanks in all circumstances."* This verse tells us to be thankful in every circumstance. Every circumstance?

When I was diagnosed with cancer, I was grateful. Why? Because it was caught early. In every circumstance, give thanks.

If you have a roof over your head, give thanks. Don't focus on what you don't have. Give thanks that you have a warm place to sleep in the winter.

A recent newspaper article reminded me of this. Social workers in a nearby city had been notifying the homeless who camped along the river that their makeshift tents and lean-tos would be dismantled soon. Some of the tent residents had already moved to a shelter while others were still hanging on to what little they had.

If you have more than enough, give thanks, not just on Thanksgiving Day, but for each day that God has given you. Giving thanks in every circumstance should leave your cup overflowing. Mine is.

Acknowledge the giver of blessings. Watch your cup overflow.

Don't forget to K.I.S.S.

"This will be a sign to you: You will find a baby wrapped in cloths and lying in a manger." Luke 2:12

Do you know how to K.I.S.S.?

I do. However, it's taken me years to learn. To keep it simple, that is.

A small newspaper item caught my attention recently because the headline was titled "Local Church Reminds People to KISS." K.I.S.S. is an acronym for Keep it Simple, Stupid. The church, however, was offering a one-day workshop to encourage people to keep it simple and sacred during the holiday season.

To remind everyone that Jesus is the reason for the season, the church was providing ways to have a simple and sacred Christmas celebration. Kids were invited to bring an adult and make a snowman Advent calendar. Adults also had the opportunity to buy an alternative Christmas gift from Heifer International.

I can remember trick-or-treating for UNICEF, an organization that benefits children worldwide. The organization still exists but you don't hear as much about it today.

What you do hear, even before the stores have cleared their Halloween merchandise, is the sound of Christmas bells. Somewhere between the scary costumes and the artificially decorated trees, we have forgotten to give thanks.

In our rush to start celebrating a season that has become too commercialized, we are caught up in the flurry of secular activities. What would Jesus think?

In the past decade, I decided to be more like Mary who sat at Jesus' feet, instead of a Martha, stressed with her preparations for Jesus' visit. I don't want to criticize Martha because I used to be one. Having the perfectly decorated tree and house, rushing to one holiday activity after another and stressing about the perfect gift left me so frazzled, I couldn't enjoy the season.

A recent phone conversation with a friend reminded me of this annual scenario. She said, "This year I'm not going to run around trying to make everything perfect for my family, even if they demand it. I'm going to enjoy this time with family and friends, remember the real reason for Christmas and keep it more holy."

What if each one of us made that choice? Wouldn't it be awesome?

I love this time of the year—the smell of a freshly cut tree, the sound of the Salvation Army bells, the taste of fruitcake, the sight of twinkling lights—but I dislike the advertising blitz that leaves you feeling like you've been run over by a runaway sleigh full of intoxicated elves.

I'm not a Christmas grinch. I love seeing the smiling eyes when a gift I have chosen brings joy to a loved one or friend. It's the greatest present I receive at this time of year.

Why not start a new tradition this year? Set a limit on your spending and stay away from more credit card debt. Avoid the malls and enjoy just being with your family and friends. Better yet, make your own gifts.

Remember God's Son and our Savior. He's the sacred reason for this season.

Finding Hope in the Small Things

"Now faith is being sure of what we hope for and certain of what we do not see." Hebrews 11:1

I watched him shuffle across the parking lot of a local home improvement store. As usual, I was in race-walking mode.

I slowed, however, when he called out to me: "If I could, I'd challenge you to a race." There was a smile on his handsome, wrinkled face.

I couldn't help myself. My hurried walk to the double doors was forgotten as I changed course to meet this delightful gray-haired gentleman. During our conversation, I learned that doctors believe he is in the beginning stages of Parkinson's. There is no cure.

Again, I couldn't help myself. I asked his name, gave him a hug and made a promise to him: "I will put you on our prayer list at church."

Inside the store, I turned back one more time and asked if there was anything I could do to help him with his shopping. He told me no, but said, "You are a beautiful woman."

I thanked him and had to laugh when he replied, "I'm not flirting with you. I don't want to give you the wrong impression."

My impression of this brave soul was one of hope. I didn't know what had brought him to the store that day, but I knew in my heart that he would keep putting one foot in front of the other until his legs would no longer carry him where he needed or wanted to go. Even then, something told me that he wouldn't give up hope.

A friend and I were recently discussing how her business has grown over the past year. She has worked hard to achieve her goals. Like me, she has so many things she still wants to accomplish that if she lived three lifetimes, she would still not get everything done. But we have hope.

For those who struggle to put food on the table, clothe their families and pay the bills, the sight of an overnight 10-cent jump in gas prices can lead to despair. They are looking for hope.

After the devastation of Hurricane Katrina last year, many struggled with finding hope among the ruins of what was once their life. A group of Houston mothers, wanting to help the children who had been evacuated to shelters there, provided paper and crayons for them. As one mother said, "Give a kid a crayon and they're going to use it."

The Katrina Kids, as they became known, found hope through the expression of art. Their first drawings were dark and frightening. With time, the images turned brighter, revealing the transformation that had taken place.

Like my elderly gentleman friend, you have to start from point A to get to point B. That requires hope and placing one foot in front of the other.

How can you package that? How could you place a price on it?

You can't. However, God did. That hope came in the form of a tiny package born over 2000 years ago.

Tupelo or Bust

"For I know the plans I have for you, declares the Lord, plans to prosper you and not to harm you, plans to give you hope and a future." Jeremiah 29:11

I gawked as my car passed the rusty truck with a crude wooden rack surrounding the bed. I thought I was on the set of the "Beverly Hillbillies." I wasn't sure about the make and model of the vehicle, but it sure looked like the Clampett's 1921 Oldsmobile that I passed one day on HWY 66 headed to Tulsa.

The truck bed was loaded with furniture and other miscellaneous items. Rope secured their belongings. Attached to the tailgate was a cardboard sign with the words "Tupelo or Bust" and Jeremiah 29:11 scrawled in bold, black letters.

Because I did not want to forget the Bible passage, I asked my son to write the chapter and verse in the notebook I carry with me. I was eager to get home and find the exact wording of the citation.

When I searched for Jeremiah 29:11 in my NIV Bible, I read: "For I know the plans I have for you, declares the Lord, plans to prosper you and not to harm you, plans to give you hope and a future."

As I pondered this verse, a visual image of the dilapidated truck came to mind. Heaped on the back of that vehicle was probably everything the occupants owned. It wasn't much but the owners had carefully tied their belongings down.

I had no other clues about the passengers of the jalopy. I wondered about their journey. Who were they? What was their situation? When had they embarked on their pilgrimage? Where had they started? Why Tupelo? How had their choices led to the current decision to pack up and move?

I would have loved to sit down with these travelers. I wanted to ask them so many questions besides the ones above. I have always been curious, wanting to know more about people and the choices they make. Maybe that's why I chose journalism as my college major.

Then I remembered the other part of the sign posted on their truck: "Tupelo or Bust." Curious, I went to the town's website and read the following: "Tupelo is truly Mississippi's 'All-American City.' It's the place to go for small town friendliness and big city attractions. Situated in the heart of the Mid-South, cradled amid the gentle rolling hills of Northeast Mississippi, Tupelo is a city that thrives on success."

Although it didn't answer all of my questions, I understood more about the brave pilgrims headed down the highway to Mississippi. They have faith. Their hope in the future is manifested in the Bible verse: Jeremiah 29:11.

We could learn a lesson from these travelers who had taken a giant leap of faith when they packed their meager possessions and headed to Tupelo with the assurance that God had plans for their future. Their hope was revealed in the hand-written words from Jeremiah.

My hope is in the Lord. Is yours?

Love Without Limits

Love is patient, love is kind. It does not envy, it does not boast, it is not proud. It is not rude, it is not self-seeking, it is not easily angered, it keeps no record of wrongs. Love does not delight in evil but rejoices with the truth. It always protects, always trusts, always hopes, always perseveres.
1 Corinthians 13:4-7

Wouldn't it be nice if love were like a cafeteria line? When I read this opening question in one of Max Lucado's daily devotionals, I thought, "Wow, wouldn't that be nice?"

Picture yourself going through a cafeteria line, selecting those qualities that appeal to you. Just like we select the food that appeals to our palate, we could select those characteristics in a person that we most appreciate and pass over those aspects that we don't especially like. For me, it would be like avoiding the brussel sprouts and tofu. Give me that apple pie with vanilla ice cream instead.

Let's see, if I were searching for traits in a potential mate, I'd take a large bowl of humor. Oh, and I must have a huge platter of handy man. I can't miss the side plate of humble pie but I'll skip the helping of moodiness.

Think of the choices we could make if we could go through the cafeteria line of love. What if we could do this with our children? We could select those qualities that we consider important, like good grades and no temper tantrums. We could avoid the tumultuous teen years and the messy bedrooms.

However, what if our children could go through that same smorgasbord line and pick out the parental qualities they considered loving? I'm sure we wouldn't be surprised at their choices. Let's see: "Give me a heaping plateful of allowances, a nice car and a cell phone, but forget the rules and losing my driving privileges when I miss my curfew."

If love were like going through a cafeteria line, it would be great. But what if someone were going through that line looking at your qualities. I know that some of my less lovely attributes would not be something you would want to savor. I'll pass on Carol's tendency to chatter too much and skip the nagging when people don't pick up after themselves.

If we could select those qualities that most appeal to us and ignore the rest, would it be love? What if God chose to not overlook our less lovely qualities? We'd all be in trouble. But God loves us unconditionally.

I recently came across the Serenity Prayer but with a new twist:

"God, grant me the serenity to accept
the people I cannot change;
The courage to change the one I can;
And the wisdom to know that person is me."

When "love without limits" is our choice, we are emulating the master of loving. When He is our guide, we don't have to worry about the choices we make. He has already made them for us.

How to be Happy

"Happy is he whose help is the God of Jacob, and whose hope is in the Lord his God." Psalm 146:5 (NLV)

Someone once asked me what made me happy. Without hesitation, I replied, "Helping others."

Many people are searching for happiness. Most fail in their quest because they are looking in all the wrong places. They're trying to find it in someone or something outside of themselves.

A relationship with the Lord is the foundation for happiness. When we build on that foundation, then we can fully experience happiness. I recently came across the following list of Ten Rules for Happier Living:

1. Give something away.
2. Do a kindness.
3. Give thanks always.
4. Work with vim and vigor.
5. Visit the elderly and learn from their experience.
6. Look intently into the face of a baby and marvel.
7. Laugh often—it's life's lubricant.
8. Pray to know God's way.
9. Plan as though you will live forever—you will.
10. Live as though today is your last day on earth.

When you reflect on these rules, you also realize that they don't require money. They are not complicated. They don't come with a list of additional steps. Nor do they come with a list of ingredients that you have to buy at the store. Anyone can follow them.

Over the past few years, I have made an observation about people who have lived into their 80s and beyond. I am especially fascinated by those who have celebrated their 100th birthday and more. I want to know their secret because, God willing, I plan to live that long too.

Their secret? It's not just in the genes. Nor is it just a healthy lifestyle. They have followed some or all of the ten rules listed above.

A 104-year-old Kansas man was recently recognized as "America's Oldest Worker," an honor given to him at a ceremony in Washington. Ralph Waldo McBurney still goes to work at his honey business every day. Waldo attributes his longevity to three things: he never smoked nor drank, he ate his vegetables, and he keeps very busy. (See rule #4 above.)

Another centenarian, Rosella Mathieu, is 100. In addition to being an active herb grower, she has been keeping a journal of her journey through her later years and is contemplating writing a book of her experiences as a guide to others. "It's hard to get answers to questions you have as you get older," she says. "I think that's one thing I can make a contribution on." She cares passionately about others, particularly as they enter the uncharted territory of life after 80. (See rules #2, 5, 9 and 10.)

I recently struck up a conversation with an 83-year-old gregarious woman while shopping at a bookstore. I learned that she would be celebrating her 84th birthday that week. When I told her that she didn't look her age, she replied, "That's because I have Jesus in my heart."

With Jesus in your heart and a heart for others, you can't go wrong. Happiness will be yours.

But He's My Son

"Those who know your name will trust in you, for you, LORD, have never forsaken those who seek you."Psalm 9:10

When the phone rang, I wasn't prepared for bad news. My oldest son had been seriously hurt in an accident. Life Flight was transporting him to an emergency room.

As I raced to the hospital, my cell phone became a lifeline to my friends. My request was simple: "Please pray for my son."

My heart ached but my eyes were dry until the family was allowed to see him. Tubes inserted into his body snaked from machines that beeped and blinked. Needles poked into his pallid flesh, contrasting with the paler sheets that covered his lifeless body. Blood was everywhere. I choked back sobs for this grown man, my son, the father of my grandchildren.

What would happen to his children, his wife if…I didn't want to think about it? I wanted him whole and healed. Repeatedly, I prayed, "Lord, don't let him suffer. Don't let him die."

While watching the machines that were helping my son to breathe, I recalled his childhood injuries that oftentimes had forced a quick run to the doctor or emergency room for stitches or a cast. He was only three when he sustained his first broken bone.

This time was different. I could not kiss the wounds and reassure him that everything would be okay. I was not the all-powerful mother who could fix it with a band-aid. But my God could, if He would. My son's life was in His hands. My silent prayers kept vigil over my unconscious son. Minutes seemed like hours. Hours seemed like days.

As I paced through the hospital corridors seeking solace in movement instead of stillness, I paused to read the comforting words on a framed piece of artwork: "God is our refuge and strength, an ever-present help in trouble." Psalm 46:1

The words of the psalm penetrated my heart and served as a message from God. My anxiety faded. I felt God's touch. I knew He was near, reassuring me that His love was sufficient for me. Filled with peace, I continued my prayer-filled walk through the halls and back to my son's bedside.

When my son finally awoke and responded to questions with a nod or a shake of his head, gratitude forced tears down my cheeks. "Thank you, God. Thank you." Those two simple words did not seem adequate to express my gratefulness to a loving Father who spared my son—a man who is almost as old as God's son when He died for us.

I have often wondered how God could sacrifice His son for my sins. Without question, I could easily give up my life for my son's, but how could I ever sacrifice my son? I couldn't.

However, a loving Father did. He gave up His Son for me. A loving Father offered up His Son for mine. A loving Father parted with His Son for you.

His Son paid the price so that we might live forever. "Thank you, God. Thank you."

Welcome to the Crowd

"The apostles said to the Lord, "Increase our faith!"
Luke 17:5

"I have faith. I just want proof to back it up." Those words, spoken by an actor in a movie I watched recently, reminded me that many of us struggle sometimes to have faith.

Unexpected expenses cause bills to pile up on our desk. A loved one is diagnosed with an incurable disease. A job loss leaves a father wondering how he will support his family.

Life experiences can cause our faith to expand and deflate like a hot air balloon. Have you felt that way? I know I have.

Have you felt at times that your faith is shrinking instead of growing? Welcome to the crowd. Even Jesus' disciples knew they needed more faith. They begged Him, "Increase our faith!"

When I read this passage, I realized that even those who were closest to Christ didn't exhibit super faith or impeccable behavior. However, they knew what they needed, and they asked.

A friend, who has overcome many life disappointments, shared an encouragement which she hands to friends and strangers, along with a small rock. On the blue card is the following inspiration from Mark 11:22-23: "Have faith in God," Jesus answered. "I tell you the truth, if anyone says to this mountain, 'Go throw yourself into the sea,' and does not doubt in his heart, but believes that what he says will happen, it will be done for him."

Instructions on the card read: Please follow directions as needed to conquer your mountain! When you feel defeated, put your rock on the floor in front of you. Stand on it. Now you have conquered it.

If it stands in your way, with your rock on the floor, walk around it. There is always another way.

If it bothers you, kick your rock to the side. Then cast it away, because you will not walk in offense. Now pick it up. You have done the impossible. You have moved a mountain.

This is your mountain. God said to move it. You just thought it was bigger.

This rock was once a boulder. This boulder was once a mountain. Remember, mountains are only as large as you see them.

Some people read Mark 11:22-23 and get frustrated because they have faith and the mountains don't seem to be moving. We can believe and we can try but sometimes that mountain won't budge.

When I wanted to build a flowerbed, I had to move rocks. Some were part of my plan; others were not. Sometimes the rocks were heavy and could only be moved one at a time. I felt frustrated because I seemed to be making little progress. Hours later, I stood back amazed. The mountains had been moved.

Faith still moves mountains but sometimes the greater act of faith is not seeing the mountain move instantly. We have to work with God to move it bit by bit.

What is the mountain in your life? Just ask God for more faith and watch that mountain become a pile of rocks.

Much Ado About Nothing

"Lord, I have heard of your fame; I stand in awe of your deeds, O Lord. Renew them in our day, in our time make them known; in wrath remember mercy." Habakkuk 3:2

Brittney is bald. Tom and Katie, better known as TomKat, wed after they had a child. Anna Nicole Smith, the former Playmate, is dead. Tragically, she leaves behind a five-month old daughter and a fortune that many people claim belongs to them—both the child and the money.

I ask the question, "Who cares?" I certainly don't, even though the media says I should. It is, as Shakespeare's most famous comedy is titled, "Much Ado About Nothing."

I don't really care about the lifestyles of the stars mentioned above. However, I feel sadness for them. They have wealth. They have fame. In some cases, they have a significant other. But I don't envy them.

A recent news program examined a trend among young people. The term, "fame junkie," is used to describe an obsession with lifestyles of the rich and famous. When teens were polled and asked to choose which one of the following they would rather have—beauty, intelligence or fame—an overwhelming majority selected fame. Girls, more than boys, coveted fame.

The same group was asked about career possibilities. When given the following choices: university president, CEO of a large company, U.S. Senator, Navy SEAL, or an assistant to a celebrity—not a celebrity, but an assistant— guess which one was the winner? Being a celebrity's assistant, even if it meant doing menial tasks like carrying luggage, was selected by 43 percent of the 10,000 respondents.

According to the news report, teens thought becoming famous would make their life better. One respondent said, "Fame will solve all my problems." Another one replied, "Becoming famous will make my life better."

If fame is a fix, why do so many celebrities seek attention through outlandish stunts, get in trouble with the law or experiment with drugs? Seeking to fill the emptiness that fame can bring with its wealth and notoriety, they are searching for meaning in their glamorous lives.

According to a recent poll, 31 percent of teenagers believe they will be famous when they grow up. Jake Halpern, the author of a new book titled, "FAME JUNKIES: The Hidden Truths behind America's Favorite Addiction," is quoted as saying, "We all covet fame, and it's how close we can get. Ideally, we're right in the center of the spotlight. It's us who are famous."

During a recent Bible study, our pastor mentioned two men in the church who had, for more than 20 years, shown up every Sunday morning around 6:30 a.m. to help get the building ready for services. Whatever needs to be done before the first service, the two are willing to do. Always available to work behind the scenes, they do not desire fame. Their goal is to serve the Lord.

Not all of us are addicted to, nor do we desire, fame. We only aspire to serve the Lord, the most famous of all.

Can't Take it with You

"For we brought nothing into the world, and we can take nothing out of it." 1 Timothy 6:7

Each weekend, especially when the weather starts to warm, signs start popping up everywhere. People are getting rid of their junk. It doesn't matter whether you call it a garage sale, a yard sale or a rummage sale, people like searching for great buys. As the old adage goes, "One man's junk is another man's treasure."

Our church recently held its annual rummage sale to benefit Heifer International. Each time we have a sale, I am amazed at the number of items donated. Like most people, we have too much "stuff."

I can recall my mother's annual sales that caused disagreements because my father didn't want to contribute anything. Mom's philosophy was "if you haven't used it or worn it in a year, it goes in the sale."

Dad didn't agree. He refused to part with any item that he might use in the future—even if it was rusty, bent, broken or obsolete.

A friend and I were recently discussing this American obsession with "stuff." She made a statement that makes sense to me. She said, "We spend the first half of our lives collecting stuff and the second half getting rid of it."

Why is that? I think, as we grow older, we realize that when we have too much "stuff," it crowds out the important things in our life, like friends and family. It also puts a barrier between our Savior and us.

One of my favorite television ministers made a good point about this issue. To illustrate her talk, she had a clothes rack on stage with a variety of her own outfits for different occasions. As she removed each one from its hanger—as if to add it to a pile of clothing she wanted to give away—she would make statements like,

"Aw, I can't part with this. I wore this 10 years ago to my daughter's wedding,"

"I'd forgotten I had this black dress. But I have so many in my closet I couldn't find it,"

"This outfit doesn't fit anymore, but I might lose weight, so I'd better keep it."

By the time she went through the rack, she realized she had an excuse for hanging on to each article of clothing that she had considered giving away. Her point? We use excuses to hang onto things that we need to let go of—not just stuff.

When our attitudes don't fit anymore, when we have outgrown our lifestyles and when we need to give up habits that hold us back from being our best for the Lord, we need to clean out our lives. We need to give it all to God and start fresh with Him.

When I think about our physical birth, I am reminded that we came into this world with nothing but the grace of our Lord. We don't like to think about death, but when I do, I remember that I will take nothing with me to the grave but His grace.

Sight Unseen

"We live by faith, not by sight." 2 Corinthians 5:7

Like most young children, my granddaughter has a vivid imagination. At times, she has been persistent that we accommodate her imaginary cat.

One night, while she was staying over at Nana's house, I had to make room in my queen-size bed for her, as well as an assortment of invisible animals that had come to visit "Cat." After moving over to make room for each new bedfellow, I wondered if I would end up on the floor before the night was over.

When my oldest son was about three, he came to the front door one day with a gift for me. Clutched in small hands was his orange sock cap. His cheeks were rosy from the cold, as well as excitement. He thrust the cap into my hands. Opening it, I expected to see…well something.

Searching inside the knit cap, I found nothing but the care label. When I looked into his expectant eyes, he smiled and said, "I caught some wind in my cap for you, mommy."

Even though my son is almost 30, I can recall the moment when with childlike faith, he placed that cap in my hands. Although I didn't see anything in its depths, I felt the love behind his gift.

Recalling my own childhood, I remember the hours I spent outdoors in the Louisiana sunshine. I didn't need evidence to feel the presence of God. I saw proof everywhere: in the magnolia trees with their large, creamy-white blossoms, in the brown pelicans whose lower bill is as long as or longer than their heads, in the swampy bayous that concealed hidden dangers but revealed a mysterious beauty with its moss-draped trees.

As adults, we sometimes find it hard to grasp something we cannot see. Our eyes demand proof. Our ears want evidence. We want cold, hard facts that we can touch. It's like being in man's court. We have to establish our innocence or refute the charges against us with some form of documentation and testimony.

What if we had been a witness on that early morning when Mary Magdalene, Mary the mother of James, and Salome went to the tomb to anoint the body of Jesus? According to the gospel of Mark, they asked each other, "Who will roll the stone away from the entrance?" However, when they arrived they found the sepulchre empty.

An angel of the Lord told the women "Do not be afraid, for I know that you are looking for Jesus, who was crucified. He is not here; he has risen, just as he said. Come and see the place where he lay. Then go quickly and tell his disciples: 'He has risen from the dead and is going ahead of you into Galilee. There you will see him.' Now I have told you."

If we were to approach Jesus' empty tomb today, would we demand evidence of His resurrection? Do we accept, sight unseen, the goodness of God and the love behind His gift? All you need is a childlike faith.

A Mother's Love

"Then Simeon blessed them and said to Mary, his mother: 'This child is destined to cause the falling and rising of many in Israel, and to be a sign that will be spoken against, so that the thoughts of many hearts will be revealed. And a sword will pierce your own soul too.'" Luke 2:34-35

She is the most well-known mother in history. She gave birth to God's son, raised Him and then saw Him sacrificed for our iniquities. As Simeon had predicted, her own soul was pierced.

Mary knew that her son was different. She had been prepared, even before His birth. But was she ready for the blood that would flow when His body was spiked with nails?

As a mother, I don't think any of us are ever prepared for what God has in store for our children. When we first hold our newborn, we anxiously count the toes and fingers. One...two...three...four...five. Yes, there are five at the end of each limb. Praise God that my child is whole!

What if your child is physically or mentally disabled? What if God has something else planned for your child? What if your child's disabilities are part of God's perfect blueprint? Can you accept that His will for your offspring is greater than you could ever imagine?

I'm sure the mother of Mattie Stepanek could never conceive what God had in store for him. In 2004, Mattie, who battled a rare form of muscular dystrophy, died three weeks before his fourteenth birthday. Mattie spent most of his life in a wheelchair and on a ventilator. However, before his short life ended, Mattie had published eight books of poetry that bring hope to the world. His writing continues to touch lives today.

A friend, whose daughter had been contemplating dropping out of college for the mission field, felt that her youngest child was making a mistake. As mothers, we find it hard sometimes to accept the choices our children make. We want to encourage them to make the right ones, yet we are sometimes fearful when they step out in faith.

When my oldest son was in his teens, he became enthralled with bareback riding. Although I was not particularly excited about his choice, I encouraged him. I knew that if I didn't, he would climb on the back of a bucking horse sooner or later. I consoled myself with the fact that at least he didn't choose bull riding. Eventually, his desire to stay on the back of a horse that was trained to dismount him waned. However, his love for horses has not.

When a serious accident with a horse sent him to the hospital a couple of months ago, my mother's heart was torn between begging him to stay away from horses and encouraging him in his dreams. The latter won out.

What if Mary had not supported her son's ministry? What if she had convinced Him to forgo the cross? A mother's love kept her at His side until the end.

Who Are You?

"Once you had no identity as a people; now you are God's people. Once you received no mercy; now you have received God's mercy." 1 Peter 2:10 (NLT)

"Dead man may have been illegal"

This newspaper headline, and the story that followed, have haunted me since I read it. The story, about a man who was found dead after falling from a train, first ran when the body was discovered without any identification. The follow-up story in the local paper revealed the man's name. According to officials, the man fit the profile of an illegal immigrant. However, none of the details had been confirmed at the time.

Two things struck me about this story. When the body was discovered, there was nothing to confirm the man's identity. Second, at this writing, his family had not been found. Unconfirmed identity. Missing family.

Several weeks ago, our pastor's sermon focused on 1 Peter 2:1-10. He opened his sermon with the following question: How would you describe yourself? Most of us, our pastor said, would immediately answer that question with our vocation: doctor, lawyer, nurse, teacher or another profession.

Six years ago, I began struggling with an important question—who am I? I could identify myself as Carol Round, high school teacher. I could also identify with the following: wife, mother, daughter, sister, aunt and friend.

However, when I was 47-years-old, my life changed dramatically. I could no longer claim the identity of wife. About the same time, my nest became empty, and although I was still a mother, and always will be, my role changed.

Three years later, I faced more changes. In the same year I became a grandmother, I also lost my mother. The following year, I retired from teaching after 30 years in the same school system. I had a major identity crisis.

When I looked in the mirror, I saw a difference in my skin and my hair color—a few more tiny wrinkles and a few more grey hairs. However, the changes I saw reflected in the mirror did not reveal my inner turmoil.

I was discussing my "identity crisis" with a friend. I said, "Who am I, Linda?" However, before she could reply, I answered my own question. "I know who I am. I am a child of God."

What about the unidentified man who fell from the train? Where had he been? What was his destination? Did he have a family?

Authorities may never know the answer to all of these questions. However, when I learned his name, I was captivated. His first name was Jesus. This reminded me of another man named Jesus.

Jesus of Nazareth identified himself as more than a remarkable teacher or prophet. He proclaimed that He was God, making His identity the focal point of His teaching. The all-important question He put to His followers was, "Who do you say I am?"

When I began to identify myself as a child of the most high God, I was no longer lost. I know who I am and I know where I'm going. Do you?

Our Father Always Provides

"Which of you fathers, if your son asks for a fish, will give him a snake instead?" Luke 11:11

When I was growing up in southwestern Louisiana, my father wasn't home very often. He worked hard in the oil-field industry. His job would take him away for days, sometimes weeks, at a time, leaving my mother to do most of the child rearing.

However, when he was home, my father spent quality time with us. My sister and I never lacked for anything. We didn't realize it at the time, but we were blessed.

Visiting with a friend recently, she commented on her deceased father, who was the pastor of a small church. He died at a young age, leaving behind his wife and five children. Because of his premature death, my friend didn't get to know her father very well.

"However, one thing I did know is that he loved the Lord and he tried to put Him first in his life," said my friend. "Since he was a minister, he had a love for people. He was extremely sensitive to treating everyone fairly and with dignity."

Although my friend's family didn't lack for life's necessities, she said that times were tough growing up in the 50s and they, like everyone else, struggled to make ends meet. "My dad wasn't afraid of work. He would haul hay and wasn't afraid to try anything."

After her father's death, times were even tougher. "My dad always told us that he couldn't leave us with great riches but he could leave us a good name. I didn't truly understand this concept until I started working out in the public and realized what an impact he had made on people's lives with his short ministry."

My friend's family struggled but "God always provided," she said, "even before we asked. It's like the story in the Bible of the woman and her son who didn't have enough oil and flour. God always replenished. My life has always been like that."

Recalling how God always provided, even when they hadn't asked, she said, "My mother hadn't worked outside the home. After my father died, she was offered a job in the superintendent's office because she was good in math and had beautiful handwriting."

The family never realized they were poor. "God provided us with work to do, like babysitting and ironing, so we could help our mother after Dad died."

As a young teen, my friend wanted to play basketball but could not afford the athletic shoes that were required for the sport. "I didn't even ask my mother because I knew we didn't have the money."

One day the coach called my friend into the hall during basketball practice to ask her what size shoe she needed. "When I told him that I couldn't afford it, he replied that someone else had paid for mine."

My friend never learned the name of her generous benefactor but she knows that "Our Father" always provides. Do you?

Finding Your Place

"Surely goodness and love will follow me all the days of my life, and I will dwell in the house of the Lord forever."
Psalm 23:6

I am not moving again! Unless, of course, God insists.

Because I have moved four times in the past six years, I have become quite adept at packing. My most recent move was less than five miles—from one neighborhood to another—but it still required finding boxes of different sizes to accommodate my belongings.

As I surveyed the pile of unpacked boxes containing my possessions, I sighed. "Not again, Lord," I thought. I had downsized once before but now found myself facing another mountain of things.

Two years ago, when I moved from one town to another, I gave away, threw away, or sold stuff that I knew I could live without. During my recent move, my routine was the same—donate, toss or sell. However, I still have too much stuff.

That stuff included an Easter basket that belonged to my youngest son, now grown. My grandchildren discovered the basket during the move. Adding to the chaotic mess, the two had scattered the fake green grass and brightly colored plastic eggs from one end of my new house to the other. It was a reminder of how much I hated packing and moving.

It also triggered a memory of the way I used to pack when I was planning a trip. My girlfriends would tease me because I never traveled lightly. Prepared for any scenario, I toted more luggage and bags than Carter has liver pills. (If you haven't heard that expression, you must be under 50.)

As each birthday passes, I realize that we go through life with too much baggage. If it's not physical baggage, then it's emotional baggage. We can choose, however, to unpack both kinds of baggage and lighten our loads. The first is easier than the latter.

For many years, I not only carried around too much physical baggage that hampered my life, I hung onto emotional baggage that hindered my growth. I was in my late 40s—not that long ago—before I began to unearth, examine, weed out and rid my life of those things that held me back from becoming the woman that God created me to be.

Until I let go of the past, I could not move on. When I was finally able to "unpack" all of that junk and dispose of it, I began to find my place in this world. However, I could not do it without the Lord's help.

A friend in my new neighborhood recently commented about emotional baggage that a relative still toted after more than 30 years. She said, "I told her that she just needed to let it go and move on."

Someday, as God's offspring, we will move to a permanent place where we will reside eternally. No packing. No unpacking. I look forward to that final move. Do you?

Monsters Under the Bed

He got up, rebuked the wind and said to the waves, "Quiet! Be still!" Then the wind died down and it was completely calm. He said to his disciples, "Why are you so afraid? Do you still have no faith?" They were terrified and asked each other, "Who is this? Even the wind and the waves obey him!" Mark 4:39-41

As a child I was afraid of the dark.

I never knew the source of my fear or how old I was when my fear led to a nightly ritual of looking under the bed and in the closet before I would crawl beneath the covers. I still wouldn't go to sleep without a night light to illuminate a small corner of my bedroom.

For years, my parents tried unsuccessfully to allay my fears of the dark. I remember waking at night and peeking out from under the sheets to see if any mysterious shadows were cast on the wall that was softly lit by the tiny light plugged into the outlet. With my little heart beating faster and faster, I lay petrified while the shadows became monsters the size of prehistoric animals.

Finally, when I could not contain my fear, I'd yell for my mother—sometimes at two or three in the morning—to ask for a drink of water. When my mother turned on the hall light, I could see that the monsters of my imagination were merely harmless moths or other night creatures.

I don't remember how many years this ritual continued, but I know my mother must have had the patience of Job to get up during the nights that I called for a drink of water simply to ease a child's fear of the dark.

As adults, we have fears of a different kind. Although we are no longer afraid of things that go bump in the night, we let other fears paralyze us and keep us from making choices—choices that could improve our lives or the lives of others.

Now, overcoming my fear of the dark seems easy compared to the apprehension I first felt when I let God lead me in a new direction several years ago. After teaching for 30 years in the same school system, I left a secure job and moved to a new community. It was faith that helped me overcome that fear of the unknown.

Fear of the unknown can keep us from taking that first step toward leaving a job and seeking another when we are unhappy or unfulfilled. Fear can stop us in our tracks when God calls us to serve Him in a different way and we don't want to leave our comfort zone.

I like Pastor Andy Stanley's statement about fear. "Fear," he says, "can drive you places you never intended to go."

Where is fear driving you? When we place our trust in the Lord, we have nothing to fear. His light will guide us from the darkness.

Searching for the Truth

"To the Jews who had believed him, Jesus said, "If you hold to my teaching, you are really my disciples. Then you will know the truth, and the truth will set you free." John 8:31-32

During the turbulent 60s, I was just entering my teen years. However, I can recall the following terms: hippie, psychedelic drugs, flower power, Woodstock and the peace symbol. It was a time—as the press described it—of free love.

A disillusioned generation of young people searched for truth. On their journey to find it, they turned to drugs and promiscuous relationships.

A friend recently admitted that in his younger years, he too, had tried counter-culture activities in his own search. When Patrick was in his late 20s, he attended an estate auction at the home of a deceased lawyer, where he purchased several items, including some boxes of books.

In one box, filled with college textbooks and tomes of the law, Patrick finally discovered what he had been so desperately seeking. However, my friend didn't find the answer he was seeking in any of the law books. He found it in a worn Bible nestled among the books. It was God's word in John 8:31-32 that set Patrick free.

Many of us spend years searching for the truth. For some, it takes decades before we discover what God is offering. We follow pop culture's wisdom, which is constantly changing, and forgo God's truth, which never changes. His truth has stood the test of time. It is as relevant today as it was thousands of years ago when it was written.

A discussion among friends recently made me realize one of the reasons we have such a difficult time finding the truth. We are constantly bombarded with media messages that tell us how we should look, think, act and dress. However, when we allow the world to define us, we give up our freedom to become the person whom God wants us to be.

A recent find at garage sale gave me another perspective. A book, by Oprah Winfrey, grabbed my attention and my quarter. The book is a collection of her "What I Know for Sure" columns. Winfrey, who has spent her life in service to others, had the following to say about truth:

"'Ye shall know the truth, and the truth shall make you free' has always been one of my favorite Bible verses—one I memorized long before I understood what it meant. I've since learned that you can't know the truth until you're willing to know yourself—and vice versa. Knowing yourself is a lifelong process, with your biggest lessons often emerging from your biggest mistakes."

During my 50+ years, I have made many mistakes. I didn't always heed those lessons. When I came to know the Lord personally, however, He revealed to me the possibilities that unfold each day in my life. I can choose to embrace those opportunities and live my life with integrity or I can keep stumbling and searching.

What is the truth of your life? Do you know where to find the answer?

When the Rains Come

"Let my teaching fall like rain and my words descend like dew, like showers on new grass, like abundant rain on tender plants." Deuteronomy 32:2

This spring, a record amount of rainfall has soaked the Midwest. In my years here, I cannot remember a wetter time. Each time I hear thunder, I think about this children's nursery rhyme:

"It's raining, it's pouring;
The old man is snoring.
He went to bed and he bumped his head
And couldn't get up in the morning."

During May and June, thunderstorms and drenching rains have caused widespread damage, and even a few deaths. Instead of praying for the moisture to make the crops grow, many have been pleading for it to cease.

I was at church one Saturday afternoon preparing for Bible School the following week. My two grandchildren were with me. I had given each a slice of pizza for lunch and left them sitting at a small table in the church nursery. I continued working with others, hanging decorations in anticipation of the children who would come streaming through the doors for VBS on Monday morning.

As we worked, thunder announced the arrival of another June storm and my grandchildren came screaming down the hallway. "Nana, I'm scared. The thunder is loud."

I scooped them up in my arms and said, "You don't need to be afraid. That's just God talking to you."

Of course, they were curious. "What is He saying, Nana?"

I replied, "Why He's telling you that He's going to send some rain."

Like most children, their standard reply is "Why?"

"To water the flowers and the grass."

"But why, Nana?"

"So they can grow."

This answer seemed to satisfy my grandchildren, who consented to return to the nursery and finish their pizza. While another VBS worker and I continued hanging decorations, I would periodically check on Cheyenne and Brennan. I motioned to my co-worker to share the moment when I found the siblings, sitting side-by-side, holding hands. With their free hand, each held pizza.

This touching scene reminded me that God will bring storms into our lives. Sometimes, those storms are gully washers that threaten to sweep us off our feet and into the unknown. When that happens, we must remember that He is always there to hold our hands and see us through to the rainbow.

In the Bible, the rainbow is a symbol of the covenant between God and man, and God's promise to Noah that He would never again flood the entire Earth. He didn't promise us days without pain, laughter without sorrow or sun without rain. But God does promise us strength for each day, comfort for our tears and a light for our path.

While we are enduring the thunderstorms of life, God can use those times to help us grow—if we allow Him to. His word will sustain us like the rain that nurtures the flowers and plants in the fields.

What storms are you facing today? Turn to the Master of storms. He'll see you through.

Pulling the Weeds

"It is for freedom that Christ has set us free. Stand firm, then, and do not let yourselves be burdened again by a yoke of slavery." Galatians 5:1

I like weeding my flowerbeds. Some might think I'm crazy but it's therapeutic to grasp a weed with your fingers and pull it from the soil.

Recently, as I was preparing a new flowerbed, God brought to mind a comparison. Pulling weeds from a garden so the flowers can bloom is the same as ridding ourselves of the weeds that keep us from growing and thriving in God's grace. Weeds are useless, detrimental and worthless, and they can choke the life out of us.

As I was checking out at a local store the other day, the cashier commented on the phone call she had just received.

"Someone called to ask if we carried a certain brand of cigarettes," she said.

Before I could reply, she added, "I don't see how they afford to smoke. Cigarettes are so expensive."

"Yes," I said, "and they are very addictive."

Webster's dictionary defines addiction as "the condition of being habitually or compulsively occupied with or involved in something." It doesn't matter if it is cigarettes, alcohol, drugs, gambling or unhealthy food, they are all weeds that threaten our well-being.

Addiction, however, doesn't have to be a craving for something physical to satisfy our desires. We can become enslaved to other habits, like the need to be in control at all times.

I have also come to realize that things we acknowledge as "good" in our society can actually be detrimental to our health and our relationships. Consider the following phrases:

"keeping your nose to the grindstone," "burning the candle at both ends," and "biting off more than one can chew."

I confess that the last phrase often describes me. I have a hard time saying "no," especially to things I really would like to do. When I know that my gifts and talents will allow me to accomplish the task, I feel guilty if I don't comply with someone's request for help. Guilt is another weed that can threaten our garden of life.

We don't need weeds in our landscape. They are pests. We have to learn to recognize the weeds that thrive in our lives and compete with what God considers more valuable. Once we identify the weeds that are undesirable, we can start removing as many as possible. However, you have to pull one weed at a time to get to the root of the problem.

Weeding doesn't have to be backbreaking and tedious, but it requires work. As we patiently remove each weed, we make room for the "good stuff" to grow.

God wants us to bloom where we are planted. With His help, we can free our lives of troublesome weeds, break through to new ground and grow into the person He has created us to be.

Are you ready to dig? With Jesus as your partner, you can remove anything pesky that is ruining your garden.

Letting Go of Martha

"Martha, Martha," the Lord answered, "you are worried and upset about many things, but only one thing is needed. Mary has chosen what is better, and it will not be taken away from her." Luke 10:41-42

If someone who knew me ten years ago visited my house today, she would think that a different person lived here. She might find dirty dishes stacked in the sink or a basket of clothes to be folded sitting on the living room floor. If she inspected closely, she might find a fine layer of dust on my furniture.

Tasks that once seemed of utmost importance, no longer control my life. If I leave unwashed dishes in the sink, what will it hurt? If the clothes do not get folded when I remove them from the dryer, will the world stop? Will the sprinkling of dust on the furniture lead to a natural disaster?

In the past, I kept a daily to-do-list. It became the controlling factor of my days. I couldn't sleep peacefully until each item was neatly marked off the list. It really mattered to no one except me.

When I taught high school, sometimes my students would hide my list as a joke. They knew that my missing agenda would put me in a state of panic because I couldn't function without it—or so I thought at the time. What if I forgot to take care of an important task on my list? What if there was a deadline and I missed it?

Being a perfectionist does not guarantee happiness. I was striving to meet high standards in every area of my life. My efforts compelled me to work harder to achieve the next level of perfection—at least in my eyes. No one noticed if I had overlooked a small detail, but I did.

Often, we spend too much time worrying about the smaller details in life or about events that never happen. How can we let go of "our" to-do lists and follow the Lord's plans for our life? How can we let go of trivial matters and spend time on more valuable, lasting experiences that can make a difference?

I used to be a Martha, expecting perfection from myself and others. I worried more about someone finding jelly handprints on the refrigerator door than on building important relationships, including the most important relationship of all—a relationship with the Lord.

Through a relationship with Him, I have found freedom. Today, I would be Mary, sitting at Jesus' feet, absorbing all He had to offer—and begging for more. The Bible is clear that man (or woman) cannot reach perfection. Once I learned this lesson, I was free to be me.

Are you a Martha or a Mary? Don't miss out on the important things in life. Leave those dirty dishes for later and let the dust bunnies multiply under your bed. You won't regret it.

What's on your to-do-list? Does it include spending more time with the Lord?

Just Because You Go to Church

"For we are God's fellow workers; you are God's field, God's building." 1Corinthians 3:9

"I'm a Christian but I don't go to church."

That statement, made during a conversation I overheard between two women recently, grabbed my attention for two reasons: the tone of the speaker's voice and my life experiences with religion.

Almost six years ago, when I was lost, I came to know the Lord personally as my savior. Growing up, I attended church faithfully but drifted away in my early 20s. I returned to my roots after my sons were born because I wanted them to have the same foundation of faith. However, over the next two decades, my church attendance was sporadic. My excuse? I met so many hypocrites sitting beside me in the pews that I convinced myself I didn't need to be there. I thought I was above all of that.

I was self-righteous in my thoughts. I even made the same statement as the woman in the overheard conversation. "I'm a Christian but I don't go to church."

I like a statement made by one of my favorite television ministers: "Going to church doesn't make you a Christian anymore than going to McDonald's makes you a French fry."

We justify our lack of church attendance by condemning the behavior of those who do. While church attendance is not a requirement to have a relationship with the Lord, I believe that it is a necessity for our spiritual growth. Fellowship with other believers helps us along that path.

Attending church is also an act of obedience to God. In Hebrews, the writer tells us "not to forsake meeting together as some are in the habit of doing, but let us encourage one another."

Why do some people shun church? Is it because we put on our Sunday morning faces at religious services and then live the rest of the week as if we have left God behind in the building where we worshipped. If we save our best behavior for the Sabbath, what does that say about us as Christians?

I like how my pastor defines church: "A church is not a hotel for saints. It's a hospital for sinners."

We all face temptation—even those who attend worship services each week. Being part of an organized fellowship encourages us in our walk with the Lord. When one of us stumbles and falls, we have our church community to help lift us up.

When I first started writing this column, I approached numerous Oklahoma newspaper editors about carrying it weekly. I received a variety of similar responses. However, I still recall one editor's reply almost two years later.

"I really like what you have to say, but don't you think you're preaching to the choir?"

"Sometimes, even the choir needs a reminder," I replied.

Attending church is an expression of our love for God. The preaching and teaching of His word increases our faith and builds us up spiritually.

A church is more than four walls. Are you a part of it?

When Your Crayon Breaks

"He restores my soul. He guides me in paths of righteousness for his name's sake." Psalm 23:3

This time of year, I love walking through a department store's school supplies section. When the shelves are fully stocked, I find myself wandering down the aisle, wishing I were going back to school. For 43 years, I did—if you count my 30 years of teaching.

I associate a school year with newness, an opportunity to start fresh. There's nothing like opening a new box of crayons. So many different colors from which to choose, even more today than when I was a child. The paper wrapped around each slim cylinder sports names like periwinkle, burnt sienna, maize and thistle. I still favor the original colors: red, blue, yellow, green, brown, black, purple and orange.

For some unknown reason, young children like to peel the paper from the crayon stick. Recently, I observed my grandchildren as they sat quietly on the floor coloring in one of the many books I have purchased for them. My granddaughter, who is 19 months older than her brother, became upset when he started removing the wrapping from a yellow crayon.

"Stop it, Brennan," she ordered in her best bossy big-sister voice.

Brennan just kept peeling away. After one more order from his sister to cease and desist, Brennan retaliated by snapping the crayon in two. His sister was not happy.

"Nana," she yelled, "Brennan is breaking the crayons."

She didn't realize that I had been quietly observing the unfolding scene and was prepared to intervene. However, before I could respond, Brennan said, "I'm sorry, Hi-Anne."

His two-year-old vocabulary, while very sophisticated for his age, cannot quite enunciate the syllables needed to pronounce "Cheyenne." I watched as Brennan tried to restore the crayon to its original glory. He pushed the two pieces of yellow together, determined to make them whole again. Frustrated, he kept pushing until another piece broke off. He finally realized that it was beyond his capability to fix the crayon. Looking up at me, he said, "Nana can fix it."

While I explained to my grandson that I could not restore the yellow crayon to wholeness, it made me realize how often in life we make a mess of things and try to fix it on our own. No matter how determined we are to fix something that is broken, especially relationships, we cannot make them whole without help.

I know the ultimate healer of brokenness. He may not restore our crayons, but He can restore people. I remember a song from my youth. The words go something like this, "Only love can break a heart, only love can mend it again."

When Jesus walked the earth, He spent time in healing and teaching. His motive? Love.

When we turn to the healer of broken hearts and broken lives, He can restore us. Even though I walk through the valley of the shadow of death, I will fear no evil, for He is with me. His rod and His staff bring comfort.

The Road to Success

"Do not let this Book of the Law depart from your mouth; meditate on it day and night, so that you may be careful to do everything written in it. Then you will be prosperous and successful." Joshua 1:8

For 30 years, I was an Oklahoma public school teacher. Since my retirement two years ago, I have come to realize why I stayed for three decades—for the teenagers who shared their joys and sorrows and allowed me to become a part of their lives.

I became eligible for retirement at the end of 2004, which meant leaving in the middle of the school year. And even though you won't find "retirement" mentioned in the Bible, I was ready to retire. I felt that after 30 years I was being led on a different path.

However, as the deadline approached to submit the necessary paperwork, I hesitated. I didn't have the inner peace that comes when one knows that it is the right thing to do. One morning, I lifted up my concerns to the Lord. My simple prayer was "Heavenly Father, where can I best serve you?"

Immediately, I felt as if someone had lifted a backpack of rocks from my shoulders. My steps became lighter because I knew I didn't have to struggle. God would show me the way.

Later that week, I had a conversation with a substitute teacher. She was a retiree, but had never substituted in the high school until that day. I mentioned my indecision about leaving at Christmas. When she replied with "Carol, you need to finish what you started," I knew that God had provided my answer.

I started the second semester with excitement, not even counting the days until the last school bell rang. Two weeks before school ended, a student, struggling with decisions about the future, approached me with her concerns. She was lost. I understood. I had been in her shoes before I found the Lord.

During our conversation, I shared with Stephanie how God had changed me from the inside out. I also gave her a copy of "The Purpose Driven Life." It was at that moment when I realized why God had wanted me to finish what I had started in August 1975.

My retirement check is not much but the rewards of being allowed to touch lives is something that money cannot buy. God crowns faithfulness even when the world has a different definition of success.

I like how Ralph Waldo Emerson defined success: "to laugh much; to win respect of intelligent persons and the affections of children; to earn the approbation of honest critics and endure the betrayal of false friends; to appreciate beauty; to find the best in others; to give one's self; to leave the world a little better, whether by a healthy child, a garden patch, or a redeemed social condition; to have played and laughed with enthusiasm, and sung with exultation; to know even one life has breathed easier because you have lived— this is to have succeeded."

What is your definition of success?

Get Out of the Box

"Ah, Sovereign LORD, you have made the heavens and the earth by your great power and outstretched arm. Nothing is too hard for you." Jeremiah 32:17

"Out of the box" has become a popular catch phrase, including "thinking outside of the box."

The term derives from a famous puzzle created by early 20th century British mathematician Henry Ernest Dudeney. The puzzle, consisting of nine dots in a three-by-three grid, challenges those who try to interconnect the dots by using four straight lines without the pencil leaving the paper. In order to be successful, the puzzle solver has to realize that the boundaries of the dot array are psychological. The only way to solve the puzzle is to extend the lines beyond the artificial boundary created by the nine dots.

After my relocation several months ago, I asked a friend to help me decorate my house. I like her taste in décor because it is similar to mine and because she has artfully arranged her own possessions. Melissa has a talent for rearranging, reorganizing and redecorating using the items on hand. A nationally syndicated television program calls it "Design-on-a-Dime." I call it saving money.

As Melissa went from room to room in my home, she studied what I had available in my collection of photos, artwork, knick-knacks and other décor. After placing various items on the floor, she arranged them in different ways to get the most appealing results. I had given her carte blanche to do as she pleased with my things.

When we finally finished—six hours later—I was amazed at the transformation she had made with my collections and keepsakes. I was also surprised by the everyday ordinary items she used as substitutes to achieve the desired results. Simply amazing.

God's like that too. He can take everyday ordinary people and use them to achieve His desired results. However, we have to be willing to allow Him to transform us so that He can use us for His purposes. That means we have to get out of our boxes.

When asked to speak at a women's retreat this fall, I agreed to do a small group session. The request came from a woman who belongs to a different denomination than mine. She said, "Carol, you will be a first for our church."

When I asked her what she meant, she replied, "You will be the first one outside of our denomination to speak at our retreat."

Without thinking whether I was stepping on toes, I replied, "God doesn't care whether you are a Methodist or a Baptist. He just wants to have a relationship with us."

She replied, "You're right, Carol. We need to get outside of our box."

We need to realize that we can't put people in a box anymore than we can put God in a box. He can do anything. So can we—with His help.

Another definition for "out of the box" comes from the Australian slang for remarkable or exceptional. When we get out of our boxes, God can do remarkable things through us. Are you stepping outside your box?

Treasure the Unexpected

"The kingdom of heaven is like treasure hidden in a field. When a man found it, he hid it again, and then in his joy went and sold all he had and bought that field." Matthew 13:44

As I sit quietly, I listen to the soft snores of my 81-year-old father. The stillness is punctuated by the sounds of the early morning hospital routine.

I use the time to read my Bible. Along with other members of my church, I am studying the parables of Jesus. This week's lesson is from Matthew 13:44-46.

In both parables, Jesus' message is the same. It is, however, the Bible study insight into Matthew 13:44 that had led to my early morning reflections. Using the term, "serendipity," the author illustrates the parable for the reader's deeper understanding.

According to the dictionary, serendipity is the gift of finding valuable things unexpectedly. In Matthew 6:33, Jesus says, "But seek first his kingdom and his righteousness, and all these things will be given to you as well."

As I write, I am experiencing a valuable gift in an unexpected place—the hospital room where my father may be spending his final days. The night before his surgery was an opportunity for us to share laughter as he told stories about his youth, his years in WW II and other adventures during this journey called life. Some stories I have heard; other tales are revealed as Dad realizes his time is near.

In his lifetime, my father has experienced things that I will never know. Growing up during the Depression years, he was the youngest of four boys. Although times were tough, his hard-working parents always managed to provide for their sons.

I recall a serendipitous moment six years ago when my father and I were sharing a meal at a restaurant. I could see tears forming, ready to spill, when he said, "Carol, you remind me so much of my mother."

It is those moments that I will always treasure. As my father's breathing becomes more labored, each word that he manages to speak is like gold to my ears. Even while in pain, his humor is a reminder to me that good things can be found in unexpected situations.

In the future, I will be able to recall these precious moments. Mixed with tears will be laughter as I share with others the joy I have found and the lessons I have learned in a hospital.

Another day is dawning. As I reread my Bible study, I contemplate more of the author's insight into the parable of unexpected treasures. To experience serendipity, one must be open and alive to the moment and responsive to what life is offering now.

I don't want to let my father go. Neither do his other loved ones. When the time comes, he will leave behind many people who were touched by his life.

When we turn aside and look closer, we can find God's kingdom—even in a hospital room where a loved one is dying.

The Measure of Our Days

"Lord, let me know my end, and what is the measure of my days; let me know how fleeting my life is."Psalm 39:4

It's 8:30 a.m. My hand wants to reach for the phone and automatically dial 918-253-4457 as it has at this time each day for more than three years. It had become part of a ritual since my mother's passing.

This time, however, there will be no one to answer my call. If I were a few minutes late, his gruff voice would greet me with "I've been sitting here waiting on you," or "I thought you had forgotten me this morning."

"Never, daddy," I would reply.

How could you forget someone like my daddy? He was a people person, collecting friends like a stamp enthusiast searching for the rarest of stamps. He was, himself, a rare man indeed. However, he wasn't perfect.

Although my grandmother Lillie had raised her four sons in the church, I'm sure she had to use a little coercion to get them there. I think she probably had to drag my ornery daddy, the youngest, by the ear sometimes.

When I was a child, I discovered a Mason jar full of Sunday school pins for perfect attendance. Grandmother had saved the mementoes for my daddy. When I asked him about them, he replied, "She made us go to church every Sunday, even if we didn't want to go."

After WWII ended and my daddy returned home, I don't think he set foot in a church, except for weddings, including his own, and funerals. He always said the roof would fall in if he did.

Preceded in death by his parents, his siblings and my mother, my daddy was always vital and full of life. He lived to spend time with his great-grandchildren. However, this year when he turned 81, his health began to fail.

He spent the last two weeks of his life in a hospital where staff members fell in love with my daddy. As long as he was coherent and aware, he had a smile, a wink, a gleam in his eye or a teasing word for each one who came into his room.

He knew his days were numbered. During one of our morning phone conversations, several weeks before he was admitted to the hospital, he said, "Carol, I think the man upstairs is calling me home."

"Why do you say that, Daddy?" I asked.

"I just know," he said.

He did know. More importantly, I know that one day I will see my daddy again. A week before his death, he made peace with the Lord. That inner peace came from knowing that no matter what his sins, the Lord Jesus had died for him.

Our life on earth is fleeting. But when we accept the eternal life that we have been offered, our days never end. Daddy had wanted to live long enough to see his great-grandchildren attend college. He will. It will just be from a different view—a heavenly one.

Your Guaranteed Inheritance

"And you also were included in Christ when you heard the word of truth, the gospel of your salvation. Having believed, you were marked in him with a seal, the promised Holy Spirit, who is a deposit guaranteeing our inheritance until the redemption of those who are God's possession—to the praise of his glory."Ephesians 1:13-14

A dozen or so blue chambray shirts hang in my daddy's closet. Some are faded and threadbare. Others had been worn only once, maybe twice. The newer ones were recent birthday and Father's Day gifts.

As my sister and I bagged up his clothing to donate to charitable causes, we put some favorite pieces aside for relatives and friends. We both realized the finality of our actions. Daddy wouldn't be wearing his faded overalls or the Levi's with red suspenders anymore. An assortment of creased and dirty cowboy hats, both felt and straw, would be divided among his grandsons. A few hats, still in their boxes, looked like new. He only wore them on special occasions.

My father's death, while not expected, was inevitable. He had been healthy for 79 of his 81 years. Any health issues he had faced were minor compared to what my mother suffered before her death three years ago.

Several months before my mother's passing, she mentioned several possessions that she wanted given to family members. As she made her wishes known, I spoke up concerning a small chair that had been given to my daddy when he was five-years-old.

"If I do not get anything else," I said, "I want daddy's little chair."

My father responded, "Go ahead and take it now."

I did.

120

I'm not sure why that small wood chair means so much to me. It's just a simple chair designed for a small child's bottom. Paint of various hues is splattered across the chair back as if a mischievous young artist decided to decorate its plainness.

My mother revealed to me how the chair had been used as a stepstool when she needed to reach something out of range of her 5'4" height. She admitted having stood on the woven seat to paint kitchen cabinets, which explains the splotches of pale yellow and green. Eventually, the seat, worn through with age and misuse, had to be replaced.

As my father approached his mid-seventies, he was kind of like that chair. He needed knee surgery to replace the ones with which he had been born. My father entered the world in 1926. In 1931, he received a gift of a sturdy brown chair. The piece of children's furniture is not fancy. No intricate carvings grace its exterior. It would not fetch a fortune if it were sold at a yard sale, an antique auction or on EBay. But in its simplicity, it is a reminder to me that the greatest inheritance we can ever receive was not bought with silver and gold.

The price of our eternal inheritance was paid for with the blood of a perfect lamb. Are you ready to accept your guaranteed birthright?

When God Says No

"Do not be anxious about anything, but in everything, by prayer and petition, with thanksgiving, present your requests to God." Philippians 4:6

"Because I said so." That was the standard reply when my sons wanted something and I had told them "no," usually more than once.

I've heard my oldest son using the same tactic when my grandchildren persist in their pleas for an affirmative answer. I'm sure I learned it from my parents, as my son learned from me. Maybe it just comes naturally for us parents, especially when we don't take the time to explain the consequences of letting our children have their way each time they beg and plea.

Sometimes, however, we have to learn a lesson the hard way. My grandchildren spent the night with me recently. My queen-sized bed is always crowded with the addition of a two-year-old and a three-year-old. Before the night is over, I usually relocate to the living room sofa to seize a few hours of sleep without a small hand smacking me in the face or a tiny foot kicking me in the back.

With their recent visit, I was reminded of how persistent a child can be sometimes. As we were getting ready to go to the park before lunch, my granddaughter rummaged through my vanity drawer to find a comb or brush. Her hair, like mine, is thick and curly. She had settled on a small round brush when I told her that it was not a good choice for her hair.

"Cheyenne, you'll only have a tangled mess."

"Why, Nana?"

"That brush is not made for use when your hair is already dry," I replied.

"But why, Nana?"

"Because I said so."

I was getting impatient because I also had to deal with her younger brother who had begun pulling things out of another drawer, including lipstick. I could just see him writing on the walls. I rescued my makeup and began to comb his hair.

Cheyenne ignored my warning. Before I realized what she was doing, she had her long locks twirled tightly around the brush. I knew it would take scissors to free the mess. I tried unsuccessfully to remove the brush without pulling her hair. Tears flowed down her cheeks as she pleaded, "It hurts Nana."

Before I began snipping, I called her daddy. When I told him what had happened, he said, "Are you sure you can't get the brush out?"

When I told him I had tried, he replied, "Go ahead and cut it if you need to but I don't think her mother will be happy."

Laughing, I said, "Cheyenne isn't very happy either."

As parents, we sometimes grow weary of our children's questions, including the "but why's?" Our relationship with the Lord can be like that too. Like small children, we want to know why. We ask for understanding. We can ask, "Why, God, why?"

Some things only God knows and sometimes his answer is no. Do you trust Him, the creator of all, to know what is best for you?

Printed in the United States
203748BV00001B/373-423/P

9 780937 660454